SURFING ADVENTURES
OF THE '60s, '70s
AND BEYOND . . .

*To Wyatt
Stay Stoked
brother.
Andy Forsyth '23
It's about the ride*

SURFING ADVENTURES
OF THE '60s, '70s
AND BEYOND . . .

Andy Forsyth

Copyright © 2009 by Andy Forsyth.

Library of Congress Control Number:		2008909394
ISBN:	Hardcover	978-1-4363-7940-3
	Softcover	978-1-4363-7939-7

All rights reserved. No part of this book may be reproduced or transmitted in any form or by any means, electronic or mechanical, including photocopying, recording, or by any information storage and retrieval system, without permission in writing from the copyright owner.

This book was printed in the United States of America.

To order additional copies of this book, contact:
Xlibris Corporation
1-888-795-4274
www.Xlibris.com
Orders@Xlibris.com
50654

Contents

Contents 5
Acknowledgements for
    Songs 9
    Poems 11
    Illustrations, Paintings, Photographs 11
Preface 15
    Special Thanks 16
Author's Biography 21
Author's challenge to the readers 27

Chapter 1: Hey Andy, Let's Go 31
Chapter 2: Where's My Surfboard? 38
Chapter 3: Bodysurfing Otter 45
Chapter 4: Sign of the Times 50
    A Little Surfing History 56
Chapter 5: What is a Surfer? 58
    Surfing Etiquette 66
Chapter 6: Types of Surfers 70
Chapter 7: How Old Do You Have To Be? 78
Chapter 8: Flat Waves, Fog, and Rainy Days 85
    Flat Days 85
    Surfin' in the Fog 86
    And in the Rain 86
    Ashes Falling 89
    Big Waves, Cold Water 90
    Grey Suits 91
    Tennis Shoes 93
    Changes in the Wind 93
    The Grunion are Running 94
    Dune Buggy 94
    Surf Movies 95

Chapter 9: Hot Dogs and Marshmallows 97
Chapter 10: Parties, Girls, Horseback Riding, Bicycling 104
    Sunset on the Beach 104
    Parties Anyone? 105
    Beach Parties 106
    Motorcycle to the Beach 107
    The Graduate Movie and Horseback Riding 109
    To The Beach 110
    In the Army 111
    Bike Ride to the Beach 111
    Crutches at the Beach 112
    Tow-in Skateboarding 112
Chapter 11: Hitchin' a Ride 115
Chapter 12: Traffic Jams, Near Misses, and Close Encounters 119
    Encounter with a Rambler 1964 119
    Traffic Jam Going to Work 120
    To the Beach, Not Quite 120
    Parking Lot Encounter 121
    Bending Hoods 1966 121
    Changing Lanes 122
    Totally Engulfed 122
    Left Turn, Stop 123
    Loose Surfboards on the Freeway 124
    Leaking Valve Stem 124
Chapter 13: Staying in Surfing Shape 126
    Skateboarding and other Sports 126
    Lifesaving 127
    Weight Lifting 128
    A Gallon of Milk 128
    Basketball or Baseball 129
    Handball and Racquetball 129
Pictures, Paintings and Drawings 131
Chapter 14: Oh, That's Gotta Hurt 163
Chapter 15: When You Gotta Go 167
Chapter 16: Red Water and Smokey Skies 169
Chapter 17: Surfin' in the Snow 171
Chapter 18: Safe Water or Not and Bad Air 176
Chapter 19: Motorcycles and Surfboards 179
Chapter 20: Over The Huntington Pier 183

Chapter 21: The Wedge 189
Chapter 22: Turn Left 193
Chapter 23: Stop the Car 198
Chapter 24: No School Today 203
    Senior Ditch Day 203
    Anyone for Golf? 205
    Orange Groves and Smudge Pots 205
    Stuck on the Mountain 207
    Baseball Day Off 207
Chapter 25: Full Moon Night Surfing 209
    Part I, Day Surfing at San Clemente 209
    Part II—Night Surfing at San Clemente 214
Chapter 26: Shake Rock 'n' Roll 217
Chapter 27: Interesting Characters and Famous People 223
    Jeff Clark, Big Wave Surfer, Mavericks 223
    Buddy Ebsen, Actor 224
    Rodney Forsyth, My Grandfather 225
    Edmund Shumpert, Artist, Surfer 226
    Steve Smith, Musician, Songwriter 227
    Marty Hogan, Professional Racquetball Player 228
    Reuben Gonzalez, Professional Racquetball Player 228
    Charlene Tilton, Actress 229
    Other Famous People 230
Chapter 28: Absolutely Nothing to do with Surfing 232
    Football, New Years Day 232
    Up to Mt Baldy on a Motorcycle 233
    Fishing at Lake Arrowhead 234
    First Airplane Flight 235
    Catamaran 236
    Rolling Down the Sand Dunes 236
    After a Basketball Game 237
    Three Months of Freedom Left 238
    Rose Parade 240
    A Road Called ZZYZX 241
Chapter 29: Things You Must do as a Surfer 243
Chapter 30: Surfing Locations 263
Chapter 31: Places I've Surfed 275

Author's Final Note of Thanks 277

Acknowledgements for Songs

	Chapter
The Beach Boys	
All Summer Long, (Brian Wilson, Mike Love)	-10
Alley Oop, (Dallas Frazier)	-3
California Calling, (Al Jardine, B.Wilson)	-5
Catch a Wave, (B.Wilson, Love)	-7
Do It Again, (B.Wilson, Love)	-26
Girls on the Beach, (B.Wilson, Love)	-23
Hawaii, (B.Wilson, Love)	-4
Melekalikimaka	-17
Noble Surfer, (B.Wilson, Love)	-5
Santa Ana Winds, (B.Wilson, Al Jardine)	-19
South Bay Surfer, (B.Wilson, Carl Wilson, Al Jardine)	-16
Still Surfin, (Love, Terry Melcher)	-20
Summer in Paradise, (Love, Melcher, Craig Fall)	-10
Surf's Up, (B.Wilson, Van Dyke Parks)	-4
Surfer Girl, (B.Wilson)	-10
Surfers Rule, (Wilson, Love)	-24
Surfin', (Wilson, Love)	-2
Surfin Safari, (B.Wilson, Love)	-1
Surfin USA, (Wilson, Love)	-4
The Surfer Moon, (Wilson)	-25
Wipeout (with words)	-9
Jan and Dean	
Ride the Wild Surf	-8
Sidewalk Surfin' (with The Beach Boys)	-10
Summer Means Fun	-22
Surf City (with The Beach Boys)	-11

Other Musicians

California Sun—The Rivieras	-10
G.T.O.—Ronny and the Daytonas	-22
I Live for the Sun—The Sunrays	-10
Little Honda—Hondells	-10
Surfer Joe—The Surfaris	-6
Surfin' Bird—The Trashmen	-14

Instrumentals

Balboa Blue—The Beach Boys	-21
Hawaii Five-O—The Ventures	-4
Let's Go—The Routers	-1
Let's Go Trippin'—Dick Dale	-11
Out of Limits—The Markets	-10
Over the Wave—The Beach Boys	-20
Pipeline—The Chantays	-4
Stoked—The Beach Boys	-20, 25
The Lonely Surfer—Jack Nitzsche	-6
Theme from "Endless Summer"—The Sandals	-20
Walk Don't Run—The Ventures	-8
Wipeout—The Surfaris	-9
Witchi-tao-to—Harpers Bizarre, Brewer and Shipley	-10

Recent Songs by Trop Rock Artists

Permission has been granted by the musians for each of these songs.

Gone Surfin'—Gary Seiler	-1
Heart of a Beach Town—Scott Kirby	-8
I Dreamed I Was a Beach Boy, Too - Sunny Jim	-20
Lucky Man—Scott Kirby	-25
Slow Down Summer—Rob Mehl	-9
The Sun Never Comes Up—Scott Kirby	-8

Gary Seiler: http://www.garyseiler.com/
James "Sunny Jim" White: http://www.sunnyjim.com/
Rob Mehl: http://www.robmehl.com/
Scott Kirby: http://www.scottkirby.com/

SURFING ADVENTURES
of the '60s, '70s and beyond...

Poems　　　　　　　　　　　　　　　　　　　　　　Chapter

(These are the beach and surfing poems I wrote except for the two by Dan and Diane as noted.)

A Beautiful Memory, Dan Brown, 1970	-7
A Dream Come True, 1973	-preface
A Floating Island, 1969	-4
A Time for the Sea and Me, 1972	-20
An Amazing World, 2006	-17
And The Waves, 1979, 1995	-8
Come Again, 1973	-2
Free As a Day and Night, 1969	-25
Helms Bread Truck, Diane Wakoski	-1
Highway 1 Junction 10, 1969	-5
Nowhere in Particular, 2005	-6
Onward I Surf, 1973	-3
Onward Seagulls, 1973	-23
Raindrops of Life, 1972	-8
Sailing We Will Go, 2007	-15
Something Simple, 1975	-24
The Old Man Wonders, 1970	-5
Warm Places, 1969	-10
We Felt the Summer's Sun, 1973	-31
Which Way Does the Wind Blow, 2005	-9

Illustrations, Paintings, Photographs

Permission has been granted by each of the following individuals for use of the images that appear throughout the book. Most acknowledgments are given with the image. If there is no acknowledgment then it is the property of the author.

Steve Wilkings, photographs; Bruno Turpin, paintings; Garry Birdsall, paintings; Jane Forsyth, drawings, photographs, painting; Ashley Forsyth, drawing; Brad and Colleen Forsyth, photographs; Marilyn Estep, photographs; other photographs are the property of the author; some images were from internet open sources.

In loving memory of:

Leila Margaret (Starks) Perry (GG)—my grandmother—1903-1995
Cecelia Anne (Perry) Forsyth (CeCe)—my wife—1946-2005

Preface

The premise of this book is to give the reader a glimpse into what it was like to be a young surfer in the 60s and early 70s. These are the stories of what happened to my surfing buddies and me but more importantly they are the stories and adventures of the everyday surfer, the guys and gals who were out there going to the beach enjoying being young and living the lifestyle of that time period. Everyone who surfed or went to the beach has similar stories to tell. Over the years I've shared my surfing stories with people, listened to amazing stories from some wonderful people and also some real characters where you would find it really hard to believe their stories. These are our adventures, experiences and the crazy things we did.

I hope you enjoy this book and find it entertaining, a little funny, reflective, and that it sparks your memories of the past. Perhaps this book will inspire you to start watching surf movies again, read more books and magazines about surfing or go on your own surfing safari, take pictures or actually go surfing, if you are able. I really just hope it makes you smile a little and remember that magical time when we were young and surfing in the 60s.

It has been a blast writing this book and recalling all the wild, crazy, strange and funny things that happened. I tried to keep the writing simple and the dialogue minimal and as realistic as I could to portray what really happened. I never imagined in my wildest dream when I was growing up that I would be writing a book about all the crazy things we did or that happened to us while we were surfing. I remember at one point when I was riding my bicycle to the beach to go bodysurfing that it felt like I was in a movie and that it wasn't really happening. It would be really wild if this all was turned into a movie or a TV series like **That 70's Show**. They could call it **That Crazy 60's Surfing Show** or something like that.

Special Thanks

I'd like to thank the many people for making this book happen. First of all I'd like to thank my parents, Lloyd and Jane Forsyth, for whom none of this would have been possible, which goes without saying. Their tolerance and understanding and forgiveness of me during those crazy and wild times will always be appreciated. Also their advice, even though not always taken, was understood. I knew what they meant and what they were saying. I just had different ideas of what I wanted to do.

My mom did several of the drawings that appear throughout the book and she took a few of the photographs that appear and had kept them all these years, thank you so much. In the past, she has designed a couple of cover illustrations for poetry books that were written and published in the 50s and 60s by my late aunt, Pegasus Buchannan. She also clarified a couple of events that I didn't have quite correct. My niece Ashley Forsyth, my brother Chris' daughter did one of the drawings also. I'd also like to thank my brother Mike for taking the time to make some editing suggestions as well. Many thanks to Bruno Turpin, (France), for allowing me to use some of his amazing paintings throughout the book. *www.surfarts.com*. Garry Birdsall, (Australia), is the artist who painted the front and back covers of the book. He also designed the title of the book. Many of his paintings are included in the book as well. Check out his web site: *www.surfart.com.au*. These two artists just mentioned can also be found in the web site "The Club of Waves", *www.clubofthewaves.com*. Steve Wilkings', (Mission Viejo, California), photographs of surfers and beach scenes from 1964 through 1970 also appear throughout the book. He too has a wonderful web site with thousands of photographs of people surfing, wind surfing and all kinds of beach activities. His web site is *www.stevewilkings.com*. And finally Marilyn Estep, my fiancée, who listened to my stories and made suggestions about how to present some of the stories, songs and poems.

Of course thanks to all my surfing buddies who unknowingly are the characters (i.e., victims) in this book. I hope I didn't offend anyone but I only used first names or a different name to protect the innocent or guilty. (But then I went and put your high school picture in the book, hopefully you look totally different now so no one will recognize you.)

My Grandmother GG, Leila Perry, for her guidance, loving friendship, and for just being the sweetest person I've ever known. My Grandfather Oliver Harold Perry, even though he wasn't around a long time in our lives had a special influence on us. My other grandmother, Nina Forsyth—who loved her grandchildren and her collection of "owls and cats"—was also a poet and a wonderful grandmother to us. And then my other grandfather, Rodney Forsyth, who is included as one my most interesting characters. He was a great person and was always willing to help me when I would show up unexpectedly.

My three brothers, Chris, Brad, and Mike who were great younger brothers growing up and who I still remain very close with even though they live in California and I live in Maryland. My brother Mike wrote a book called **Revelations**, based on the book in the Bible and he helped me with some writing and publishing ideas and tips. Of course, my loving wife of thirty-three years, Cecelia Anne Perry Forsyth, the first love of my life, who I lost in 2005. She was an amazing, determined, unselfish, and loving mother and wife. She got to see me surf in Hawaii in 1973 on our first anniversary and honeymoon (since we didn't have one right after we were married) and also at Leo Carrillo State Park in California a week later, then again the last time I surfed in Ocean City, Maryland, in 1985. My sons Matt and Dave, who I love and are both very important to me. They are great sons and put up with listening to my surfing stories hundreds of times over the years.

I'd liked to extend a special thanks to the staff at Cheeseburger in Paradise, in Pasadena, MD, (A Jimmy Buffett affiliated restaurant) for allowing me to spend countless hours composing and typing this book into my laptop at their establishment. Most of this book was written while eating their food and listening to the piped in Island Trop Rock music, live bands (sometimes they even played some Beach Boy songs), or watching football games on Sunday and Monday nights. I'd like to especially thank John Sparkman, the proprietor and general manager for taking an interest in the book and encouraging me and listening to some of the stories as I was writing them.

Sounds like a song in there somewhere

I was in Key West this year (November 2007) and was telling the story of our trip to Mexico (about when I asked the clerk at the liquor store "How old do you have to be to buy beer?") to Dennis McCaughey and Randy Zimmerman of the Trop Rock group "Tropical Soul" and Dennis's wife Sue who is also the band's manager (www.tropicalsoul.net). They got a big laugh about that story and Randy commented, "Sounds like there's a song in there somewhere." I hope they write the song because they are very talented songwriters, musicians, and performers and would do a great job with it. We hired them to play at my birthday party (July 2007) at Cheeseburger in Paradise. John enjoyed them so much that he's hired them a few times to play again since then.

How This Book Started

I was in Myrtle Beach, South Carolina, on vacation, sitting in the Margaritaville Restaurant—also a Jimmy Buffett affiliated restaurant—and the idea hit me to write this book. I had been watching the movies ***Riding Giants, Stepping Into Liquid, Mavericks, Endless Summer,*** and ***Endless Summer II*** over the years and also a lot recently. I was impressed and inspired by the stories that went along with all the surfing especially those in the ***Endless Summer*** movies because not everything that happens to surfers happens at the beach; but sometimes, just getting to the beach can be a wonderful experience or an interesting challenge.

So I was sitting there with my fiancée, Marilyn Estep, who is an amazing person and the second love of my life. She could tell I was thinking about something and asked me if everything was alright. "Yes," I said, "I think I'm going to write a book." She asked, "About what?" I'm sure she was a little nervous but also curious. When I told her it was a book about all my buddies' surfing adventures, you could sense her excitement because she's heard me tell many of the stories that are in this book. She has been very supportive during this process. This is my first book and hopefully not my last. I wrote a short story a few years ago called "The Last CBK" which is a story about a man (Richard Dreisen) and his racquetball racquet, an Ektelon CBK. It was published in the "Maryland Washington Racquetball Association" (MWRA) local newsletter a few years ago and then again a year later in the online version of the "National Racquetball Magazine."

Poems and songs throughout the book

Also included in this book are about twenty poems that I've written over the past 40 years (some of which I have put to music) that reference the ocean or surfing.

SURFING ADVENTURES
of the '60s, '70s and beyond...

You'll also see many lyrics of the songs about surfing throughout this book that relate to the story, however loosely, if at all. I'd like to acknowledge the following artists or groups who either composed or performed these songs:

> The Beach Boys, Jan and Dean, The Sunrays, The Rivieras, Ronny and The Daytonas, The Surfaris, The Ventures, The Trashmen, The Chantays, The Markets, The Sandals, The Routers, Harpers Bizarre, Dick Dale and Jack Nitzsche. Also included are six songs from Trop Rock artists who have written their songs recently: Rob Mehl, Gary Seiler, James "Sunny Jim" White and Scott Kirby.

All of the beach songs we'd listen to on the way to the beach, while we were at the beach, or just driving around in our car. These songs were at the heart of the surfing experience back then and gave us an identity. Every time I hear a surfing or beach song today, it takes me back to a time in my life that I will never forget and wish I could relive all over again or as the Beach Boys song says just "Do It Again."

But for me and probably most of us who lived during that time, the best we can hope for is to relive that time in surfing movies, in songs, or hopefully books like this one. This book is about, the everyday surfer in their youth and surfing prime, enjoying the freedom that surfing gave us. We were out there just surfing, enjoying the waves, the beach, and sharing good times with good friends, getting into trouble, sometimes working, or occasionally going to school.

A Dream Come True

To surf in the sunlight
And run along the beach
Into the waves until the sun goes down
Is the dream I dreamed last night

Many nights go by
When the sun sets like this
But I wonder as I dream
When I will go surfing again

The ocean with its roaring
Surfers gliding on the water
The moon is smiling on us all
And I dream, this dream, each night

Someday I'll live this dream
Wherever it takes me I will be
On the shores of the ocean surfing the waves
A dream that one day will come true again

Andy, 5/9/1973

Author's Biography

photograph by Marilyn Estep

Born and raised in Pomona, Southern California during the 50s, 60s and early 70s. Served in the U.S. Army for three years from 1971 to 1974 in the Washington D.C. area. Met his wife while in the Army and after being discharged from the service attended and graduated from the University of Maryland in 1976. Then started a career in the field of Computer Sciences.

During the next 30 years he was helping to support his family and raising his two sons. The memory of his wife and all her love and support during their 33 years of marriage will always be appreciated and never forgotten. Especially putting up with listening to me talk about surfing and other sports all the time.

A little background about the Author (by the author)

    I enjoyed going to the beach with my family on our vacations and would notice people standing up on large boards while being pushed along on the water. It looked like fun but I didn't really know what they were doing because I was too young. Eventually when I understood that what they were doing was surfing I became interested in it and was hoping to one day give it a try. The 60s ushered in the beach and surfing music by the Beach Boys, Jan & Dean and numerous other groups. The music, along with all the beach and surfing movies of the time, only helped to spark our interest in surfing.

    By the mid 60s I finally got a chance to try my hand at surfing while on a beach trip with some friends and found out it wasn't as easy as they made it look. After countless hours of determination and many wipeouts I finally stood up and caught my first wave. Even though it was the soupy white water it still felt pretty neat. After that I couldn't get enough. I'd go as often as I could especially on nice weekends and during the summer. Then a group of guys at school were talking about going to the beach to go surfing and so one day we all went on our first surfing trip together.

    The title of the book "Surfing Adventures of the 60s, 70s and Beyond" is about our adventures, experiences, misadventures and the wild, crazy and funny things that happened to us during the 60s and early 70s when we were going to the beach and surfing. The part "and Beyond" refers to not only a few other time periods and places other than Southern California but a few funny things that happened that had nothing to do with surfing.

    While in High School I began writing poetry and have written about 300 poems over the years. Some of the poems have been about the beach or surfing. I've included about 20 of these poems throughout the book as well.

    I graduated from Pomona High School in 1969 (all my surfing buddies went to PHS) and then attended Cal Poly College, Pomona for 2 years majoring in Aerospace Engineering. I'd arrange my schedule so I would either have a day off or an afternoon off so I'd be able to go to the beach and go surfing if I didn't have too much homework or if I wasn't working.

SURFING ADVENTURES
of the '60s, '70s and beyond . . .

Unfortunately for my days of surfing the Army got me in late 1971 until I was discharged in 1974. I met my future wife while I was stationed at the Pentagon in early 1972 and we were married in August of the same year. In August of 1973 we went to Hawaii for our Honeymoon/First Anniversary where I went surfing for the first time since going into the Army. Then a week later I surfed in California at Leo Carillo State Park, (for the last time) while we were on a family vacation.

After I was discharged from the service I attended the University of Maryland, College Park and received a BS Degree in Computer Science. I've worked in the Computer field for over 30 years now. I've always kept up my interest in surfing and in 1985 I tried surfing in Ocean City, Maryland for 2 days during one of our family vacations to the beach. After just 20 minutes out on the waves I found out how good of shape you have to be in for surfing because I was exhausted. It took about 10 minutes of sitting out there on the board to get the strength back in my arms to where I felt I could continue. I had been lifting weights, swimming, playing racquetball and running all along. In fact I was training for the Marine Corps Marathon that year so I felt I was in pretty good shape. But not for surfing. I was able to catch a few waves and get up but the rides were only about 4 or 5 seconds long. Not like some of the rides you get in California and Hawaii of 20, 30 seconds or longer. But it was still fun. This was the last time I went surfing. I've always done a lot of body surfing and boogie boarding while on our family trips to the beach. I would teach my sons to body surf and boogie board on our beach trips. My youngest son, Dave, keeps after me to teach him to surf so I'm hoping to get him out there some day. He's learned how to snow board and ski with me and he is an excellent snow boarder so I'm sure he'd pick up surfing fairly quickly.

Since graduating from College I've mostly been working, supporting and raising a family, coaching youth sports and playing, softball and racquetball. I've been playing racquetball since 1980 and have participated in nearly a hundred tournaments over the years. I wrote a short story about a man and his racquetball racquet entitled "The Last CBK" that was published in the local newsletter for the Maryland Washington Racquetball Association and then later it appeared in the online version of the National Racquetball Magazine.

This is the first book I've written although I have started a couple of other books, did the outlines, a little research and took down some notes, and roughed out a few chapters but they never got off the ground. Maybe someday I'll complete them, who knows. This book basically started out as just a few short stories and then I'd think of a few more stories. I'd be laughing about some of the funny things we did while I was writing the stories so it was pretty easy to write. Perhaps everything didn't happen exactly as I remember it happened but it is difficult to remember everything so I took a few liberties to make it interesting, to flow better or to be a little more humorous. But for the most part every story is true and pretty much happened the way I've told it.

Artists Biographies

Bruno Turpin, artist

www.surfarts.com

"Nulla Dies Sine Linea"
Born in Granville in Cotentin, France, Bruno Turpin has the Ocean in genes with a marine Breton fisherman father. The quays of the port he knows, it breathed them all its childhood. However these are not the boats that Bruno started to paint but the Ocean and his waves. Those also breaking in Channel took him on late. But in spite of the cold and the wind of the winter, passion is full. It overflows even on the canvas where the painter replaces the surfer to plunge in the tube and to test all the magic of it. "Surfing gave me to painting again and painting enables me to share this passion with the others.

Today Bruno is 38, married, two children, happy with surfing waves and canvas, and sharing with other his way of life. Published in magazines on regular basis, he also exhibits his work in art galleries and takes part in special events.

Author's comments about these paintings:
Bruno's paintings of surfers display the essence of long board surfing with a simplicity and elegance that is truly unique and expressive. I'm pleased and happy to present these examples of his artwork throughout this book.

SURFING ADVENTURES
of the '60s, '70s and beyond . . .

Garry Birdsall, artist

Garry Birdsall was born in Sydney where surfing is a national pastime. He spent all of his leisure time as a youth on the beaches of Sydney. He was one of the pioneers of Malibu surfboard riding, and has participated in numerous Australian and world surfing events. He was the first artist worldwide to do air-brushed paintings on surfboards.

Garry's re-creation of "Surfing in the 60's" is an authentic, historical depiction of surfing scenes of that era.

His surfworks of art are genuine, handmade, limited editions which deserve to grace the walls of the best homes in Australia and worldwide. Each artwork is signed by Garry, and carries a numbered Limited Edition Certificate. Ideal gifts for the surfing enthusiast, young and old, on any occasion.

About Garry's paintings from the author:

Garry's paintings truly capture the 60s era. The cars of that time period, the long boards and the vibrant colors make his paintings stand out. I've chosen two of his works for the front and back cover of the book. Thanks Garry for sharing your artistic skills. Be sure to visit his web site to see all of his wonderful and colorful paintings and check out his surfboard artwork designs.

Steve Wilkings, photographer

The author's comments about Steve's photography:

Steve has been photographing surfers, the beach and people involved in beach and water activities since at least 1960. I am honored to include 20 of his photographs throughout this book. He has photographed all kinds of surfers and people in locations all over the world. He has photographed many professional surfers and legends of surfing during his outings. But I've chosen surfers that are less well known for this book. I have also chosen to include photographs from 1964-1970 to try to capture that time period that most closely parallels this book. His photographs are truly representative of that era. Lots of great pictures on his web site, check them out. Thanks Steve.

Jane Forsyth, artist, photographer

Her art work has appeared in poetry books in the 50s and 60s and she is an accomplished artist but has chosen to keep her artwork private and nearly all of her paintings are displayed around the home. I have one of her paintings that is of the surfing location at Leo Carillo State Beach, which appears in the book. She gave it to us as a wedding present and I keep it on the wall at my house. Her drawings of surfers appear throughout the book at the beginning of some of the chapters and several of her photographs also appear throughout. In fact the only three pictures of me surfing, she took while we were at Leo Carillo, the same place where the painting was done. Thanks Mom.

Ashley Forsyth, student artist

One of her sketches of a surfer appears in two chapters of the book. While visiting my brother in California I noticed some of my niece's sketches and thought they were pretty good, so I asked her if she could draw a guy surfing for me. Thanks, Ashley,

Author's Challenge to the Readers

This book has been a lot of fun to write and I'm very pleased to share these stories and our adventures with you and I hope you enjoy them. I'm also hoping to put together another surfing book with your help. So if you have any funny, crazy interesting or hair raising stories that you've told over the years (not just the 50s, 60s and 70s but all time periods), and would like to share with others then send them too me. I'd love to hear from you, as I've mentioned in other parts of this book. Send your stories to me at: *alf000777@yahoo.com*.

Everyone who sends in their stories, if it is used, will receive full credit, acknowledgement and compensation (to be determined later) for their stories and will retain the rights to reuse their stories as they see fit. I believe there are a lot of people out there who were surfing during the 50s, 60s, 70s and up to today that have some great stories to tell and would like to share them. I'm sure that other people would enjoy reading about your stories, I know I would. I ran into a guy this past year (March 2008) surfing at Seal Beach, California. He had been surfing since 1960. Think of all the stories he has, wow. I also ran into a young couple, Loren Camper and Field Brook, and their dog at Balsa Chica who was there from the San Francisco area on a business trip and was able to fit a couple hours of surfing into their busy schedule, he commented that he just needed the exercise. One of my old neighbors grew up in Hawaii in the 50s and 60s and has told me some of his stories and these will be in my next book. There is also a friend in our local Jimmy Buffett Chesapeake Parrot Head Club who was surfing in Florida during the same time period. The stories are out there we just have to get them in print for all to enjoy. You can find stories in all the surfing magazines, but most are about the high profile surfers, professional surfers, prominent media events or the people that make the surfing movies or that are featured in the movies. Most of these are great stories and I enjoy reading them and watching the movies. But there are not a lot of stories about us, the everyday average surfer, having fun, getting into trouble while just trying to get to the beach to go surfing, and getting away awhile from the hassles of the everyday life and really just enjoying the waves, the beach, great weather and great friends.

Surf's up and stayed stoked. Andy.

SURFING ADVENTURES
of the '60s, '70s and beyond...

Gone Surfin—Gary Seiler

When the work days done I got to head for the sun
and there's a place you can always find me.
I grab a couple of boards and call a few friends of mine
it's a quick walk down to the beach
Those summer days keep a rolling in and nothing else matters to me
You're living large when you're living life down on the beach

I've gone surfin' take me down to the beach
Got those good waves cool-rays longboards sunny days that's all I ever need
I've gone surfin' kickin' back on my beach
I've been doing it since I was a young man back in my teens

Those long board days are my favorite waves
I like to chill out and take things slow
Those sweeping turns and a footloose style, walking up and down the nose
To be out there with a couple of buds I love it when the water is warm
I got the west coast east coast Baja I call it home

Oh I've gone surfin' take me down to the beach
Got those good waves cool-rays long boards sunny days that's all I ever need
We've gone surfin' kickin' back on my beach
We've been doing it since we were young kids back in my teens

Those years we have go quickly
I hope you're having some fun
If you surf your livin' your age don't matter
Surfin' just to feel young

Baby I've gone surfin' take me down to my beach
I got those good waves cool-rays longboards sunny days
that's all we ever need
I've gone surfin' hangin' out on my beach
I've been doing it since I was a young man back in my teens

www.garyseiler.com

Andy Forsyth

photograph by Steve Wilkings

1

drawing by Jane Forsyth

Hey Andy, Let's Go

(Summer of 1969)

Beep, Beep-beep beep

"Hey Andy, it 5:30 let's go." someone yells from the car.

Instrumental: Let's Go—The Routers

I open my window and see my surfing buddies in front of my house on Kingsley Avenue in Pomona, (Southern) California, waiting for me. His dad bought an old Yellow Chevy Helm's panel bread truck for a couple hundred bucks and that's what we used for our wheels to get to the beach. In the glove box, they found the old whistle that the driver used to blow while driving through the neighborhood to let people know he was coming by. Sort of like what the ice cream trucks used to do by playing their music. There are only two seats and plenty of room for about eight surfboards and up to eight guys in the back. Plus we could put about six boards on top.

"What time is it?" I yell back.
"Five-thirty, let's go," they yell back.
"Ok I'll be right down." I said.

I already had my board on the front porch and my surfing trunks ready, sun tan lotion, some surf wax, about $20, my sleeping bag, and I was ready to go. Oh yeah, don't forget a beach towel and sunglasses. As I run out the door with all my stuff, I grab my board and jump in the back. There are already three other guys in the back: Gary, Chris and Sefo. Dave and his younger brother Ed are in front; we still have to pick up Charley and Leo. The guys are really psyched and looking for a good surf weekend. Today is Saturday; we've all got the weekend free and we're headed to Cardiff-by-the-Sea to meet a friend of one of the guys who has a house next to an empty lot a couple of blocks from the beach. We'll be camping out on the empty lot. Turns out Edmund Shumpert is married and has three kids—about three, four, and five—who don't like to wear any clothes and just take a leak whenever they gotta go, even if it's right next to where we put our sleeping bags. Edmund is a famous sculptor, artist and surfing trophy designer, who has been making surfing trophies for a number of years.

painting by Garry Birdsall

Woodie

SURFING ADVENTURES
of the '60s, '70s and beyond . . .

Surfin' Safari—*Jan and Dean*

Let's go surfin' now.
Ev'rybody's learnin' how.
Come on a safari with me.
(Come on a safari with . . .)

Early in the morning we'll be starting out.
Some honeys will be comin' along.
We're loading up our Woody with our boards inside,
And headin' out singing our song.

Come on baby, wait and see, yes
I'm gonna take you surfin' with me. (Come on along.)
Yes baby, wait and see, yeah,
I'm gonna take you surfin' with me . . .

By the time we get Charlie and Leo, it's about 6:15 in the morning and we've got a 90 minute ride, maybe longer to get to Cardiff. There are several good spots there but the best is out at the point by the cliffs. There are two sets that break and both have some nice lefts and rights about 5-8' normally and a decent curl. On the trip there, we listen to Beach Boys, Jan and Dean, the Ventures, and other surf music. There's an 8-track tape player that sometimes gets jammed when the tape sticks and we have to try and fix the tape by pulling it out and letting it roll back inside. It sometimes works but usually takes a long time of messing with it. Sometimes the tape just ends up in a big pile on the floor. Bummer, now you need to buy a new tape.

On the trip down, we have to sit on our sleeping bags because there are no seats in the back. The boards are stacked and tied on one side of the Helms truck and we are laid out on the other side, six guys in the back, bouncing around. Good thing the truck can't go faster than 50 mph or we'd go flying sometimes when we hit a bump.

There's two little windows out the back on each door just about waist high, but none on the sides, and one of the guys likes to moon girls that are right behind us. Soon after he does his full moon, you'd see the car take off past us with the girls laughing. Except for this one time when he got mooned back; in fact they drove by mooning us as they went by. It was hilarious; we thought that was a riot.

We finally arrived at the beach around 8:00 AM and found a parking spot, got our boards out, and went to check out the waves. Out of the eight of us, only four of us actually knew how to catch and ride a wave. Sefo was by far the best since he was Hawaiian and had been surfing in Hawaii since he was two. The waves are looking pretty good. The ones closest are breaking around 2-4' and the ones near the cliffs are a good eight feet or better. We can't wait to get out. We get our boards waxed and we're ready to hit the waves. The weather is great, around 80 degrees, it's mid July, a nice offshore breeze which allows the waves to hang just long enough so you can drop in and get a nice tube. Just before we were about to go out, some locals show up and I guess they like to do their own thing because they took off all their clothes and put on their wet suits. When they noticed people were looking, they just shook their long hair and stood there with their arms spread like they were showing off or something. Well, this was the first time I'd ever seen someone change in public, let alone in the middle of the beach. It wasn't so bad since I didn't really care that the two guys got naked; but the two girls that were also changing into their wet suits was another story. This definitely was a first, for all of us. We were all around 16 to 18 and would always talk about how we'd like to be able to see into the girl's locker room at school and then this happens. It was too bad the girls didn't look much different from the guys, at least from the waist up. It was kind of disappointing but funny, nonetheless. I think that's just about all they talked about all day after that. They all wanted to hang around where the girls were surfing but their boyfriends were getting kind of annoyed that they were hanging around so they left and went to another spot.

There weren't that many people out, as usual for Cardiff, and we got some really good rides and after a couple of hours of surfing, most of us headed in for a rest. The guys that were just learning were trying out the smaller surf closer in and of course they were telling some tall tales about the "awesome" waves they were catching. In reality the waves they were on were about 2-4' and they mostly just rode in on the white water after it broke. But that's what's great about surfing because the stoke you get is great if you're a first timer riding a two-foot wave of soupy white water and standing up for the first time, because now you're hooked. Or if you're an experienced surfer

SURFING ADVENTURES
of the '60s, '70s and beyond...

catching an eight-foot tube totally covered and just flying, your adrenaline is soaring and you can't wait to go out and do it again. Because someday after enough practice, patience, perseverance, frustrations, and suffering through the wipeouts, they too, will finally catch that eight-foot tube and go flying through, get spit out the other end with that adrenaline and endomorphins soaring. It's better than any high you could get from any artificial drug, more satisfying, great exercise, and it's "legal" go figure. After resting a while, we head back out for more. The waves are really kicking today and it is one of the best days we've had here.

Tonight's going to be a full moon and we're planning on going back out around 10 or 11 PM to do some night surfing. Only two of us have ever ridden at night, and I wasn't one those two, so we figure this ought to be quite an experience.

photograph by Steve Wilkings
Waxing up the surfboard

We stop at a hamburger joint to get some food and then when it gets dark the moon is out and we head back out. You can only surf at night with moonlight because otherwise you can't see the waves. We're out for about three hours before we head back in. Since I had never surfed at night before, I stayed on the smaller waves at first and eventually took some bigger waves. It was fun and I couldn't wait for the next time I'd go night surfing. Some of the guys came in with these stories of these monster waves they caught and how he was standing on the nose of the board jumping up and down to keep the nose down so he could make the wave. I didn't say much I just figured they were talking a lot of stuff. I don't doubt they caught some waves but not the ten footers they were claiming.

photograph by Steve Wilkings
Catching a nice nose ride. Tom Padaca, Malibu, 1967

internet open source
A 60s Chevy Panel Truck, similar to the Helms Bread Truck we had only ours was a cream yellow color.

SURFING ADVENTURES
of the '60s, '70s and beyond . . .

A poem by Diane Wakoski, 1964

"When I was young I remember these big yellow bread Trucks which is why I knew it was a Helms Bread Truck."

The Helms Bakery Man

The Helmsman came in a Yellow Truck
With a hard shelled top, like a beetle
Sometimes when I am in bed at night,
I remember his donuts and fresh bread,
White-sacked,
Sliding out in the smooth wooden tray.

I hear a little toot,
See the yellow truck come down my old street;
And there is the Helmsman,
Asking what I want today, as I hand him my nickel.
"A bun," I say.
And he gives me one with the moon
In white icing decorating the top.

Diane Wakoski, 1964,
Emerld Ice, Selected poems 1962-1987

A Black Sparrow Book
David R. Godine, Publisher
Post Office Box 450
Jaffrey, New Hampshire 03452
www.blacksparrowbooks.com

My note about this poem:
    This is a poem I found online about a Helms bread truck. This is only about a third of the poem; the entire poem was too long to include here. I searched for months and finally found a picture of the truck. There are lots of pictures of the old small, trolley-wagon-looking bread trucks but none of the big yellow panel trucks like ours.

2

internet open source

Where's my Surfboard?

(Summer of 1968)

Practical jokes and pranks are a way of life among friends and especially so with surfers. I guess we just have an unusual sense of humor or maybe more of a warped sense of humor would be better. Miki Dora used to play some of the craziest pranks on his friend Greg Noll. Greg Noll is famous for being one of the first people to surf Waimea Bay in Hawaii. He also made surfboards and produced numerous surfing movies. Miki used to disrupt his movies with practical jokes and it would really irritate Greg.

In the movie **The Endless Summer** and **Endless Summer II**, the surfers in both movies ended up the brunt of several practical jokes by different characters in the movies. On one of our trips to Cardiff-by-the-Sea, we were all trying to outdo each other with stories or practical jokes. Again we stayed at Edmund Shumpert's house on the empty lot next to his house. Edmund learned to surf by surfing every day for a month and then didn't surf again for about a year. He mainly learned to surf so that when he built his trophies and surfing statues, he could get a more realistic sense of how he wanted them to appear. He also did some paintings of surfers and beach scenes. He was a very talented artist. Everything he did revolved around surfing. His paintings, sculptors, trophies, it was his way of life.

photograph by Steve Wilkings
Two guys on the same wave. Jim Cubberly, Secos, 1965

Cutting up the wave. Mike Purpus, Hermosa Beach, 1970

Locked in a tube. Steve Clark, Hermosa Beach, 1969
photographs by Steve Wilkings

Surfin'—Beach Boys

Surfin' is the only life
The only way for me.
Now surf, surf with me

I got up this mornin' turned on my radio
I was checkin' on the surfin' scene
To see if I would go
And when the DJ tells me that the surfin' is fine
That's when I know my baby and I will have a good time

We're going surfin' surfin'

...

Edmund was an artist and sculptor who took great pride in his work. He was contracted by the local surfing organizations to make surfing trophies out of brass. He was also making a life-size sculpture of a surfer out of a slab of marble. To make the trophies, he first made a wax statue then poured plaster around the outside to make a mold of the statue. Then he'd pour concrete or cement of some kind into the mold and after it hardened, he'd have a hard copy of the original. Of course he'd have to trim and clean it and when it was done, he'd cover it with some type of acrylic on the outside because the next step was to make the iron mold. This iron mold would be the one he'd use to make all the rest of the trophies of this size. He made several different sizes and different styles depending on the order he'd get. To make the final product, he'd pour the brass in the mold and after it hardened he'd open up the mold and he'd have the trophy, he might have to clean up a few rough edges but he could reuse the mold over and over many times. He could even use other metal-like gold or silver or aluminum depending on the order but brass was the normal material used. I can't say that this entire process was exactly accurate because Edmund explained it to us over 35 years ago but you get the basic idea.

. . . .

Here is an excerpt from an article I found about him and his sculpting, from the Webster PROGRESS-TIMES.

The process of creating a full-blown sculpture is a painstaking proposition, requiring many steps, and great patience. He detailed the process that sounds daunting to those unacquainted with the art form.

"I make a steel skeleton that looks like a stick figure in the desired pose, then wrap it completely with burlap and plaster. It will be built up with clay, and all the details sculpted and finished," explained Shumpert. "This is called the sculpture model."

The molding is done by sectioning this model into parts and making silicon rubber molds. Melted wax is poured both in and out until a one-eighth-inch hollow copy is formed in the molds.

He said the wax copies are removed, and wax tubes and a wax funnel are put on each. They are in turn covered inside and out with ceramic mold material.

"The result is that bronze turns out hollow too. The bronze casting is done by baking the ceramic molds in a kiln at 1,650 degrees for an hour and thirty minutes... just before the bronze is melted in a furnace and poured into the molds.

To finish the bronze, all parts are removed from the ceramic molds, cleaned and sandblasted. Finally, all the parts are welded together, filed, sanded and finished. This is not for the inpatient.

. . . .

So I kind of remembered how it was done but is was about 40 years ago when he told me. Anyway he was an amazing person back then and still is. He did a statue of Duke Kahanamoku that used to reside in Huntington Beach in front of the Surfing Museum. It is now inside the museum.

As you may recall, his kids would run around the yard naked all day and peeing whenever they had to go. We got a bucket of water and poured it under Gary's sleeping bag while he was asleep; he thought that he laid his sleeping bag where the kids had peed but we didn't tell him what it really was. Later that day, we were down at the beach and the guys were out surfing and Gary had left his watch and other things on his towel. I took his watch and hid the other stuff in the other guys' things or on their towels. I actually took the watch because I was going to get something to eat at the local diner and didn't want to stay too long because I wanted to get back to surfing and was going to put it back when I returned.

Little did I think they actually would show up at the diner. Gary wasn't too happy but I explained why I had the watch so he wasn't too upset but I could see he had that look in his eyes that he was up to something like maybe he was going to get me back. I guess he must have found the rest of his stuff because he didn't say anything about that. I gave him back his watch and after I finished eating, I went back to go surfing but my board was gone; at first I thought someone had taken it. I said to myself, *Where's my surfboard?* I looked around the beach and around some cars. Ed went with me up the cliff to look for my boards and to get a better vantage point to be able to see the whole area. By the time I got to the top of the cliff, it had been thirty to forty minutes since I'd been looking and as I was looking around I saw the boards right where I'd left them next to my towel. That's when I realized what had happened, that Gary had hidden my boards and got me back.

When I got back, I decided to not say anything or act like I was upset. I just picked up my board, waxed it, and went out. I knew if I didn't say anything, it would make him more upset because then he wouldn't get any satisfaction out of seeing me upset. When I came back in, he was obviously wanting some kind of reaction and all I said was "I guess you got me back." But I was just warming up. I had to think of something good to get back at him. Ed told me later that he knew my boards were taken but that he wasn't supposed to tell me but just help me look for it. Ed is Dave's younger brother; he was just learning to surf. But he always had a good time hanging out with us.

When it came time to hit the sack, for some strange reason, Gary couldn't find his sleeping bag. He tried to accuse me of taking it but I really had no idea where it was because I didn't take it. He looked all around and started to get really perturbed, but I again told him I didn't know where it was. I didn't because Ed is the one who hid it. I had him hide it so I wouldn't know where it was. I knew Gary wouldn't suspect Ed and I think Ed kind of liked being in on the pranks. I let him stew a while longer and I told Ed when he had a chance to put it in a place that you'd know he'd find it, but not to be too obvious. He did find it eventually.

I was a little worried about what he might try to pull on me but I think he was too tired because he didn't do anything. We had a great day of surfing the next day; the waves were just perfect as usual with some nice head high swells and great tubes. Gary didn't talk much the rest of the day, at least not to me. I think that was the last time he went with us to Cardiff or other trips for that matter.

After we were done for the day while he was changing, I removed the fin from his board and hid it. I don't think he even noticed it. I was first to be dropped off. I told Dave where the fin was hidden (under the driver's seat), but I told him to tell Gary that I left it at Edmunds' house. I asked Dave to tell me what his reaction was; he was really pissed but after a few minutes, Ed was to tell him to look under the seat. I guess he realized he got had again.

Andy Forsyth

painting by Garry Birdsall
Last Surf of the Day

Come Again

*Gone to the water
To spread out my arms
Run by the shoreline*

*By the wayside
By the seashore
Longing to surf the waves
Running, walking, jumping over seashells*

*Autumn and winter have finally past
Spring is here at last
I laugh as I surf and
The wind blows to form the waves*

*Now as the sun sets
I see the day has past
Remember today as it was
And the ocean, and the sun will come again*

Andy, 5/12/1973

3

drawing by Jane Forsyth

Bodysurfing Otter

(Summer of 1969)

    Leo Carillo State Park is located in Southern California about twenty miles north of Malibu. It was given to the state by the estate of the actor Leo Carillo who was primarily a silent screen film star and also played "Pancho" in the show "The Cisco Kid." I'm not exactly sure of the circumstances as to why he donated the land but from what I've learned, he donated a large portion originally to satisfy his tax obligations. Then after he passed away, in his will, he wanted the land to become a state park, with the stipulation that the film industry be allowed to use the park for filmmaking whenever they needed it. It was also to be set up as an inexpensive camping area where vacationers could go. This was great because you had the mountain-type camping just a half mile from the beach. We would sometimes go camping in the mountains but this way, we had the beach and the mountain. That was perfect for me because I enjoyed the beach and surfing but also liked camping as well. We could do some surf fishing and catch some rock bass for diner once in a while.

Lots of surfing movies were made at Leo Carillo as well as other movies that needed a beach scene. In fact, the movie *From Here to Eternity* with Bert Lancaster and Deborah Kerr, where they were rolling around in the sand on the beach, was filmed right there in the swimmers area of Leo Carillo State Beach, the same place where we saw Buddy Ebsen, but this is a later story. This area was a little cove with steps leading down to the beach and a lifeguard stand on the cliff overlooking the area. To the south of this area on the other side of the cliffs is the surfing area. Farther to the north is another cliff, a cave, and a tunnel where you can walk through to get to the other side. Through this tunnel, you'll find another beach for swimmers and bodysurfers. There are cliffs along the beach for a few hundred feet. There was a TV special being made there one time called *Alley Oop* about a caveman. Later that year, we saw the show on TV and sure enough, that scene was in the show, albeit about a three- to four-minute scene.

Alley Oop—Beach Boys

There's a man in the funny papers we all know
Alley Oop Oop, Oop Oop Oop
He lived way back a long time ago
Alley Oop Oop, Oop Oop Oop
Well he don't eat nothin' but bearcat stew
Alley Oop Oop, Oop Oop Oop
Oh well this cat's name is a-Alley Oop
Alley Oop Oop, Oop Oop Oop

He's the toughest man there is alive
Alley Oop
Wears clothes from a wildcat's hide
Alley Oop
He's the king of the jungle jive
Look at that caveman go!

During high tide, the water gets deeper and it can get a little rough in the cove and tunnel but at low tide, you can walk through easily. The swimming area usually has pretty good waves for bodysurfing. The waves

SURFING ADVENTURES
of the '60s, '70s and beyond . . .

were mostly shore breakers that broke in 2-3' of water. We used to go to Leo Carillo State Beach to go camping during the summer for a week's vacation as a family. I would watch the guys surfing sometimes but never thought I'd actually be surfing there someday. It was a great place for the family because there was the campsite within easy walking distance to the beach. It was maybe a quarter to a half mile before you got to the cliffs of the beach, depending where in the campsite you were.

There was some seaweed on the beach so you didn't hang out there unless you were surfing. It wasn't all seaweed because we used to play some football games there in the evening. There are a lot of kelp beds farther off in the ocean and a few closer, which kept the waves down a little but this also helped them to be smoother and not so choppy when it got windy. When the swells kicked up, it would still get pretty big. The bottom was all rocks but the smooth kind mostly. There was a little channel of sand that you walked through when you were going out to surf. On the right facing out from the beach were two boulders with lots of razor sharp corals attached so it was kind of dangerous and you wanted to avoid running into boulders. One was a large boulder and in front of it, about 15-20', was a smaller one that was underwater at high tide or when a wave passed over it. The wave always broke to the right and was a nice fast wave that had a tendency to close out after a 20-second ride; but sometimes, you could make it all the way for about a minute ride.

I remember seeing this "old guy" surfing; he must have been at least 40 but he was pretty good, riding his long board. There was also a guy that would ride the waves on a kayak. On days when the waves would get bigger, like around ten feet, the surfers would have to make their takeoff almost directly at the boulder and then make a quick right turn. If you didn't make a quick right turn, you could have a close encounter with the boulder. Some guys told us of this guy who would actually go between the boulders. That would take a lot of nerve and skill. I never saw anyone hit the boulders but some of the guys told us people had gotten hurt and were pretty messed up, especially from the coral.

When I first started to get into surfing, I couldn't wait for our family vacation so I could try surfing at Leo Carillo. Finally the week arrived and off we went. We would leave around 3:00 AM so we could get in line to get a campsite. If you didn't get a site, you'd have to wait, sometimes all day, until someone checked out. It was a first-come first-served basis and there was usually a little line to get in. We'd take two cars so we could have one in line while we parked in the parking lot and hung out at the beach until we got a campsite. We usually didn't have to wait too long but sometimes it might be 10:00 AM before a spot opened up. Once we got settled in, I was off to the beach for some surfing. What a bummer; the waves were nearly flat and no one was out surfing. So I had to take the board back to the campsite and ended up hanging out at the swimming beach with my family and brothers. But we made the best of it and had a good time anyway. We did some fishing or found some guys who had a football game going.

The next day was a different story and the waves were better. I had to watch a while to get used to how the waves were breaking and where everyone was setting up. I was still learning to surf this year but still had fun and got some good rides that whole week. In fact, I felt I improved quite a bit. I made some friends during the week and a couple of times, we'd get together in the evening for a little party. I had my guitar and would play some songs and we just had a good time.

The next year, my surfing skills had improved a lot since I was going to the beach almost every chance I could—including during the winter. I was out surfing in the late afternoon and the weather was perfect and the waves were ideal—not too big but around 4-6'-glassy, breaking, really nice, and not closing out so you got a nice long one minute plus ride. I was sitting on my board when all of a sudden, I felt something brush the bottom of my foot. At first I didn't think that much of it because of all the kelp and you sometimes would feel the kelp but this was a distinct thump, so I was a little concerned and I put both feet up on the board.

A few seconds later, a head popped out of the water just a couple of feet away from me. It was a sea otter! How cool was that? Thank goodness, it wasn't a shark. The cute little guy just looked up at me. He seemed to be looking right at me like he wanted to say "Hi, what are you doing here?" I just said something to him like "Hey little fellow, whatcha doing? You scared me a little bit." He didn't seem frightened but just swam around a little. A swell started coming toward us and then all of a sudden, he took off; he was heading right in front of the big swell and swam right in the wave and started bodysurfing it in. It was just like you'd see in the movies when the dolphins or seals would ride waves. I didn't see him around after that. But later that evening, you could see a couple of otters playing in the water hauling up oysters or clams and using a rock to open them up. An otter is the only sea animal that naturally uses a tool to help eat its food.

SURFING ADVENTURES
of the '60s, '70s and beyond . . .

The encounter with the sea otter was amazing and one I will always remember. It's also something that happens to us because of the surfers' closeness with nature, that is seeing other animals—fish or birds—in and around the water and you realize that their lives depend on the ocean. It is important for us to preserve and protect the environment not only for our own surfing but for the creatures that live in the water that depend upon it. When we pollute the environment, then we all lose, but especially the animals because they lose their lives as seen by too many oil spills and other manmade and natural disasters. Part of being a surfer is your raised awareness for the ocean and the environment and the ways you can help to protect this amazing beauty of nature and natural resource.

Onward I Surf

Surfing the balmy sea
Wherever the wind will lead
Surfing to an onward shore
Searching the ocean's roar

Speaking to the wind all day
Gazing at the stars all night
Surfing with the sea creatures each day
Where will I be tonight

I can't surf a choppy sea
But sometimes a stormy sea
Where the waves are too big, and I'm
Thinking it's the end for me

But onward I go
Onward I surf
I stop—then
Onward I surf
Onward I go

Andy, 5/6/1973

4

painting by Garry Birdsall

Sign of the Times

Before we get too far along I like to give a little background and set the stage for what was happening during this time period, leading up to it and afterwards a little. The 60s was a very turbulent and uncertain time. Not only was it a time of change, tragedy, conflict, but also of great achievements. There were changes in politics, tragedies in politics, conflict of war, the Cuban missile crisis in 1962, Vietnam all through the 60s and up until about 1974. In 1969, we even landed a man on the moon for the first time. I remember watching the moon landing on TV at my friend Pete's house. When I drove home right after the landing, there was not one car on the street going from his house to mine, about 2 miles. I guess everyone was watching the moon landing.

The Vietnam-police-action-turned-conflict and later turned-war was an especially difficult time for our country. In the early 60s, most people weren't even aware that we were over there and then all the protests started in the mid 60s. So many people were opposed to the war that when the soldiers came back, they were not treated very well at all.

John F. Kennedy was assassinated on November 22, 1963, just a few months before the Beatles made their first appearance in this country. The Beach Boys had already started to make it big; Buddy Holly, The Bopper, and Ritchie Valens didn't even make it to the 60s. Folk music was making a comeback with the top groups being Peter, Paul, and Mary, The Mamas and Papas, Bob Dylan, The Everly Brothers, The Righteous Brothers, The Kingston Trio, Glenn Yarbrough, Arlo Guthrie, Ritchie Havens, and others. They were singing songs written by the old folk artists like Woodie Guthrie, Pete Seeger, Burl Ives, Huddie Leddbetter, to name a few and also introducing their own songs.

Rock 'n' Roll was big but still in its infancy with the likes of Elvis, The Beatles, The Doors, The Animals, The Rolling Stones, Paul Revere and the Raiders, The Kinks, and don't forget the beach music with the Beach Boys, Jan & Dean, The Ventures, and scores of others. Rhythm and blues branched out in many directions with soul, blues, Motown, etc. And big venue concerts started to evolve like the Newport Folk Festival and Woodstock. The hippie movement and flower power sort of took over the beatniks of the 50s and early 60s. People were experimenting with the so called mind expansion drugs, along with free love, which was spreading to all cultures and all societies in America, communes where popping up all over as well. But the adrenalin high you get from surfing is better than using any drug and it is "legal", which is even better. It's also a whole lot better for you because you are getting a great workout and you have to keep in top physical condition to surf the toughest waves. We also had some very influential movies like ***Easy Rider*** which opened the doors to not only the big chopper bikes and people wanting to travel and see the country more; but it also showed the drug side of our society and the prejudices that were still around.

With the assassination of John F. Kennedy (1963), his brother Robert Kennedy (1968) and the civil rights leader and activist Martin Luther King (1968) followed by the Watts riots, the political world seemed in turmoil as well as the instability of our civil society. The political world was changing dramatically. I was watching the California primary victory speech that Bobby Kennedy was making on TV just before he was shot. My mom had just arrived home after working all day at the voting poll station as a volunteer when she sat down next to me and a few minutes later we witnessed the events as they happened. We stayed up most of the night in disbelief as another Kennedy was assassinated.

I often wonder how different the political world would have been if the Kennedys would not have been assassinated. JFK most likely would have been elected to a second term. In 1968, RFK most likely would have been elected president and hold two terms of office and then followed by Ted Kennedy for two terms, which would have taken us to 1984 with the Kennedys as our presidents. There never would have been Lady Bird as our first Lady, Nixon and the Watergate scandal wouldn't have happened; well maybe it would have anyway, except Nixon would probably have been sent to the same jail as Agnew. Yes, Ford would not have been president or pardoned Nixon. By the way, Ford was the only president who was not elected into office as president or vice president. He was appointed vice president by Nixon after Agnew resigned. Jimmy Carter wouldn't have been president and Reagan may not have won until 1984, if at all.

Enough politics, enough war, enough music except for folk music, the Beach Boys, and Jimmy Buffett. Yes, sometime in the late 60s, a guy named Jimmy Buffett had a couple of big hits like "Come Monday" and "Margaritaville" which launched the island or trop rock music. His music is still big today and has a huge following of his music by his fans known as "Parrot Heads." Now, hundreds of groups following in the spirit of his music of the island trop rock flavor are performing all over the country. Five of the songs in this book by Scott Kirby, Rob Mehl and Gary Seiler are of the island trop rock format.

What is amazing in all of the turbulence, changing political scene, riots, war, landing a man on the moon, changes in the music, sports, the beginning of the Super Bowl, that surfing was still growing rapidly and evolving. Surfing was the fastest growing industry and sport. I guess people liked the outlet that surfing gave them because while you are surfing, nothing else matters. You can forget all your troubles for the day and enjoy the experience, escape, and maybe give yourself a new perspective and outlook.

With interest in surfing growing the world over, it became a sport people of different nationalities and in different countries could participate in and have a common bond. Surfing contests began forming and eventually professional surfing took hold. In the late 50s, there were only about five

SURFING ADVENTURES
of the '60s, '70s and beyond . . .

thousand people surfing and for the most part, they were considered rebels, beach bums, outcasts or loners. But by the mid 60s, over two million people were surfing and in many other countries, numerous new surf locations were being discovered all the time. Besides Hawaii, California, some East Coast spots, South Africa, Mexico, and Australia, people weren't surfing anywhere else.

Instrumental: Hawaii Five-O—The Ventures

Instrumental: Pipeline—The Chantays

By the mid 60s, people from many other countries were getting involved in surfing and new locations were being discovered all the time. Traditionally, Hawaii was more accepting of surfing where it was considered a recreational activity, except for the more challenging big wave spots like Makaha and the North Shore where there is the Pipeline, Sunset, Waimea Bay, and many others. California surfing in the 50s and early 60s was still a relatively unknown or eccentric sport until the advent of the Beach Boys music, the Hollywood surf movies and the "real" surf movies produced by the surfing community. The most famous being, of course, **The Endless Summer**, which is probably solely responsible for the explosion of surfing in the 60s and beyond. This motion picture showed that surfing could be found just about anywhere in the world even where there wasn't supposed to be any waves, like Tahiti. And that anyone of any skill can enjoy surfing and have fun.

Today people are surfing everywhere, like in the middle of the ocean off a reef, an island in the middle of the Pacific, surfing waves in the frozen waters of Alaska or the Arctic with ice chunks floating around, off the wakes of tankers in the Gulf of Mexico or the Michigan Lakes. You can find a standing wave in a river or giant waves 30-70' plus just north of Maui at Peahi, or Teahupoo, Tahiti, or the Dungeons in Australia, or Mavericks at Pillar Point near Half Moon Bay, just south of San Francisco, and many others where you have to be towed in by a Jet Ski. Some of the guys are using hydrofoil fins on the bottom of the surfboard to rise above the water and get a gliding effect and not be affected by the turbulence of the waves. There are dozens, or maybe nearly a hundred manmade wave locations and numerous indoor surfing parks.

Hawaii—Beach Boys

Do you wanna go
Straight to Hawaii
(Hawaii) Hawaii (Hawaii)
Straight to Hawaii (Hawaii, Hawaii)
Oh do (Honolulu, Waikiki) you wanna come along with me
(Do you wanna come along with me)

Now I don't know what town you're from
But don't tell me that they got bigger waves
Cause everyone that goes
Comes back with nothing but raves

And pretty soon this Winter
They'll hold the surfing championship of the year
Surfer guys and girls
Will be coming from far and near

Go to Hawaii . . .

Personally, I prefer surfing near a beach where I can walk or take a short drive to the beach, paddle out, catch some descent sized waves, relax on the beach, and then drive home the same day or walk back to the beach house or campsite. I admire the guys and gals who search for the waves in those remote reefs and islands and I thoroughly enjoy watching the films and DVDs but I don't think I would want to do that kind of traveling all the time. But who knows, when you're young and totally into a sport, you always want to raise the bar and try to get to the next level.

Today people are surfing all over the world on all types of waves and getting there any way they can. There are lots of great "real" surfing movies being created and available for purchase. Some of the ones I have enjoyed watching are of course **Endless Summer, Endless Summer II, Riding Giants, Stepping into Liquid, Laird, Billabong, Mavericks, 100 Ft. Wednesday, and Condition Black.** There have been some good

SURFING ADVENTURES
of the '60s, '70s and beyond . . .

Hollywood movies that feature surfing but that usually isn't the main part of the movie. Movies like **Blue Crush**, which features girl surfers, **Big Wednesday, Point Break,** even a James Bond movie had a big wave surf scene in it, **Snakes on a Plane** also had some surfing in the beginning and end, **Orange County, Lords of Dogtown**, and numerous others. The animated penguin surf movie **Surf's Up** was pretty cool and was a big hit.

Surfin USA—Beach Boys

If Everybody had an ocean
Across the USA
Then everybody'd be surfin'
Like California

You'd see 'em wearin' their baggies
Huarache sandals too
A bushy bushy blonde hair do
Surfin' USA

We'll all be planning that route
We're gonna take real soon
We're waxin' down our surf boards
We can't wait for June

We'll all be gone for the summer
We're on safari to stay
Tell the teacher we're surfin'
Surfin' USA . . .

So through it all—the turbulence, assassinations, the political problems, a possible looming nuclear war with Cuba and Russia, the Vietnam conflict turned war, the changes in the music scene, the hippies, the drugs, the evolution of sports, advances in communication, computers and television, landing on the moon, space exploration—surfing has thrived, expanded, and survived its own ups and downs and the ever changing sign of the times.

A Little Surfing History:
Skimboards, Bodysurfing, and the Wedge

When I was young, I used to watch some of those Hollywood surfing movies but I never thought I'd actually try surfing until I saw someone surfing when I was camping at the beach while we were on a Boy Scout camping trip.

I saw these guys riding the waves and they were only a couple years older than me and that's when my interest was peaked. As a kid going to the beach with my parents, we used to get a small thin board and we'd use it as a skim board along the edge of the water. It was fun but we sure got a sore butt or a mouth full of sand from falling down a lot. It took a while to get the hang of it but it was a lot of fun. My dad taught us how to bodysurf but mostly he just went straight in after the wave broke in the white water. Later we learned how to ride the shoulder of a wave bodysurfing. Using fins helped a lot with being able to catch a wave better and to be able to change directions.

Surf's Up—Beach Boys

Surf's Up
Aboard a tidal wave
Come about hard and join
The young and often spring you gave
I heard the word
Wonderful thing
A children's song
Surf's Up

There are a lot of different ways to ride waves these days like windsurfing, kite surfing, tow-in on the really big waves of 30-70' plus. Some people kayak, in fact in the 60s at Leo Carillo State Beach, there was a guy that used to kayak there quite a lot. Even skim boarders venture into the shore break now to do tricks off the face of the waves. Boogie and knee boarding was just gaining in popularity and it really helped if you had fins to get better speed to make it easier to catch the wave.

SURFING ADVENTURES
of the '60s, '70s and beyond . . .

We used to go to the Wedge at Newport Beach and these waves could get up to 6-12' sometimes, you really needed fins but invariably they'd come off. There must be thousands of fins at the bottom of The Wedge. The Wedge is located at the southern most part of Newport Beach. Just across the inlet from Corona del Mar. A long time ago, they built a rock jetty to allow the boats to enter Newport Harbor without getting slammed with waves. Well this created an interesting effect with a southern swell because the waves would wrap around the rocks and nearly double up the size of the waves. If you get a Northern swell, coming in the waves would bounce off the rocks and actually travel sideways, making for a nice long ride which is really unusual for the Wedge because most rides are straight down in less than a foot of water and lasts for one or two seconds. You'd better learn how to tuck under the wave or be prepared to get bent. One morning, I got there early and saw a guy catch one of the sideways waves by jumping off the rocks with his knee board and actually stood up on the board riding a sideways wave up the beach inside the tube of another wave that was 6-8' and rode it for at least twenty to thirty seconds which had to be a record for the Wedge. Keep in mind that there was virtually nothing below him except six inches of water and sand. He made it out unscathed. I was very impressed. He's the only guy I've ever seen do this but I'm sure that others have tried it. I'd hate to see what would happen if they wiped out.

My scariest experience in the water actually wasn't surfing, although I have had my share of major wipeouts. It actually happened when I was bodysurfing at The Wedge. I've been to The Wedge numerous times, especially when I was on my motorcycle without my surfboard. I usually had fins with me but not always. On this day I went out and the waves were only 3-4' so I didn't think there'd be a problem by not having fins. There were a couple other guys out which was unusual because there are usually a lot of guys, sometimes ten or more people on one wave. Then when the next set of waves started coming in at 8-10' and I couldn't get in or out, I was trapped! The entire story is in another chapter entitled, "The Wedge."

For more history about surfing visit the following web page:

http://en.wikipedia.org/wiki/History_of_surfing

5

drawing by Jane Forsyth

What is a Surfer?

What is a surfer? What defines a surfer? Why do we surf? I guess it's only natural that some people may wonder what makes up a surfer and why we do what we do. I've read a lot of articles over the years that talk about surfing philosophy, where surfing is like a religion, or that they are soul searching. In the early 50s people thought they were just rebelling against mainstream activities or they were even labeled as beach bums. Bikers took on similar labeling as well.

Surfers are very passionate about their sport, they think it, they eat it, they drink it, they talk about it, they live it everyday. They surf just for the fun of it and to be with nature. Some people are totally consumed by it and build their entire life around surfing. I would say that there are as many different personalities associated with surfers as there are in any sport. You're always going to have the quiet ones, the soul surfers, the athletic types, the naturals, the bullies, the pros, the hotdogs, the rookies, the talkers, the ladies, which are always nice, and the kids, which are cool too. Having kids involved is important because they are the future of the sport—to keep it alive and pass it on to the next generation. Well I guess you get the idea. But a surfer is really defined mostly as a state of mind and mental attitude and that once you are bitten by the surfing bug, you're pretty much hooked.

Sparky Hudson and Crazy Kate, Hermosa Beach 14th Street, 1966.
photograph by Steve Wilkings

Most people are into bowling, tennis, golf, fishing, running, racquetball, skiing, or team sports like baseball, basketball, football, hockey, softball, soccer, rugby, or lacrosse. But a person who surfs is doing something where you are defined as a lone performer, just you and the elements. Except for the guys who ride really big waves and have to be towed in, surfers are out there challenging the elements alone. Yes there are surf teams but for the most part, they are still out there by themselves. A surfer doesn't just surf but he can be involved in multiple sports too. But there is a deep satisfaction you get when surfing that you can't get with other sports.

painting by Garry Birdsall

Beach Break

I've done a lot of thinking about what makes up a surfer and why we surfed back then and why we surf now. Probably the closest thing to surfing is snowboarding or snow skiing but you need a ski lift to get up unless you hike or climb up and you need snow and lots of it in really cold places. Surfers only need a board, swim trunks and a wave. In cold water, wet suits may be needed and are optional but almost always worn. Once you have challenged the elements of the ocean, have been wiped out and humbled by its power, and respected its beauty and grace, and are able to master the art of catching a wave, standing up, riding it in you will have finally become a surfer. But simply riding a few waves does not really make you a surfer; it has to be your passion, what you think about when you're not working, sleeping, or spending time with your wife or girlfriend and sometimes you're still thinking about surfing. But don't let your boss know or your wife or girlfriend. Also I've thought about why it is always in the back of my mind even though I haven't surfed for sometime. You end up dreaming about surfing as well, so in reality, you're thinking about surfing pretty much all the time. I haven't surfed in a long time, maybe about 20 years now, but I go bodysurfing or boogie boarding every year when I'm at the beach and before that, I hadn't surfed for about fifteen years but I still thought about surfing all the time. I watched it on TV instead of other sports, at least when it's on ESPN or other cable channels. I buy surfing magazines, books, videos, and DVDs to watch. I keep thinking that one day, I'll give it a try again, if my body will cooperate.

It really comes down to three things I believe. 1) The stoke or the high that you get. 2) Just the pure enjoyment of surfing. 3) Feeling like you are a part of nature and the environment. Let me expand on each of these a little.

1) The stoke or high is that wonderful feeling you get while you are out there on the water and after you have finished for the day and think about all the waves you were on and how much fun you had. Just you, nature and the waves. Nothing else matters during the time that you are out there surfing. It is just the best feeling you can get doing something for just the enjoyment of being able to do it and challenge yourself to accomplish something very special.
2) The pure enjoyment of the sport. No other sport or activity that you can do by yourself anywhere in the world can give you more pleasure, is physically challenging and self rewarding than surfing.

It's also not that expensive like other sports. It's not a team sport but there are surfing teams, primarily for competitions but you still are on the board alone. There are some activities that certainly come close and I'll discuss those a little later but you are doing an activity by yourself where the field of play is always changing. Skiing or snowboarding is similar but the terrain really doesn't change dynamically while you are skiing unless you're in an avalanche, then you're in deep, deep powder and in a seriously dangerous situation. Sailboard surfing is also very similar but very restrictive because of the sail and more expensive.

3) Being at one with nature. There is a peace you feel while you are out on the water waiting for the next wave. You have a chance to look around at what nature has put before us. The water, the shore, the sky, the sea creatures. There is a real opportunity to just feel like we too are part of this wonderful place for a short time. Because of that surfers tend to be environment conscious. We are out there in the elements and don't want to see the ocean spoiled or the land either for that matter. A lot of surfers are involved with environmental programs and efforts to clean up the planet from the mess that those in power before us made.

The side benefits are even better, warm sunshine (unless you're in a cold water climate), great exercise, fresh air (unless there's some smog or smoke around), and you're away from all your problems and hassles for awhile. You are part of the surfing community and we all share the same passion for surfing that you do. Anyone I've talked to who surf's feels the same way, you can hear it in their voice and see it on their faces when they talk. They are just stoked about surfing. We love to talk about surfing almost as much as we love to surf. We talk about the places we've been to surf, the beaches, the waves, the stories, lots of stories, crazy things, mishaps getting to the surfing spots or things that happened surfing or even afterwards. It's in your blood and it will never go away until you ride that final wave, then I still think, it will never really go away.

Any other solo sport I can think of either requires some equipment or devise that is expensive or is very one dimensional. Let's start with running, great exercise, aerobic, good for your heart, lungs and legs, but no real upper body benefits though. You run on the ground, it doesn't change, not like the water does. Yes you go up and down hills but it doesn't move and running is boring especially on a tread mill. Why do I think this? I've been running since being on the track teams and cross country teams in High School and even before that. I trained hard for 3 years to run in the Marine Corps Marathon in Washington D.C. between working, raising a family, softball games, racquetball, weightlifting and swimming. I ran the race in 1985 in a respectable 4 hours plus a few minutes but I finished, which was my goal. But running takes a toll on your knees, hips and ankles. And I still run because it's good for you, but it's boring.

Swimming is great exercise too, aerobic, good for the upper body and you need to swim to surf, but there are people who surf who can't swim. Gee, I hope they're wearing a floatation vest! But it too is boring, the water in a pool doesn't change and you can't stand up to swim and you need a swimming pool unless you're at the lake or ocean, then you may as well surf. Speaking of swimming pools there are also some great manmade surfing locations but it is expensive, usually fresh water, so it really doesn't count. Granted it's surfing but I'd still rather be at the beach.

Team sports are fun like baseball, football, softball, basketball, soccer, hockey, lacrosse, etc but you need lots of people to play the game. Even sports like racquetball, tennis, ping pong all require at least two people. Skiing, snowboarding, mountain boarding, mountain biking, skateboarding, bicycling, hiking, water skiing, wake boarding, the environment doesn't change or move or you need a piece of machinery like a boat or ski lift.

Golf is fun but then again it's not that much fun by yourself and you usually need 2, 3 or 4 people to play. Plus it's expensive. How about computer games? They can be fun and people spend a lot of time and money playing them. There are surfing games out there and I've even played a couple, in fact they are about the only computer game I've played that I enjoyed but come on, it's a computer game, no exercise, no fresh air, no sunshine, no computer game even comes close to the real thing.

Sky diving? Don't even get me started about this one. I'll agree it seems exciting, thrilling and fun but there's no real exercise in it. Maybe you need to be in relatively good shape but you need an airborne vehicle like an airplane to jump from. Which brings me to my point, you jump out of a perfectly good airplane that can land safely on the ground and you can walk out of it. So why would you jump out of a plane 10,000 feet in the air? It's also expensive and you need an airplane or helicopter. Now if the plane was going to crash then I'd jump and I'd pray all the way down that the parachute would open or I wouldn't land in a tree or lake. Oh I did see a thing on cable

SURFING ADVENTURES
of the '60s, '70s and beyond . . .

once where they used a snowboard and were air surfing. Pretty cool. But it's still parachuting. In surfing you don't need a parachute. Unless you're para surfing and that's expensive and really different from surfing but it looks like fun. Hang gliding or para gliding seem like fun, but expensive too. How about sailing, it helps if you have a boat and it usually requires more than one person and is fun but also too expensive. Sail boarding is really sailing but on a surfboard and you don't even paddle out. It's not really the same but it can be fun, and you don't even need waves, just wind.

Bull riding and bronco riding in a rodeo. Wow, really tough and bone crunching but you need an animal. Race car driving and motorcycle racing both lots of fun but very expensive and you need a vehicle and a team of mechanics and a bunch of other people to race against.

I'm sure I've left some things out but it still comes down to the fact that surfing is the most fun you can possibly have at a sport or anything for that matter, that is relatively inexpensive and that you can do by yourself. It's even better if you have friends to share it with. The stoke is great, the exercise is great, the physical, mental and emotional rewards are great. It's like you're part of nature and every time you surf the challenge is different. Every wave is different, no one is keeping score (unless you're in a contest, which is cool but it's not for everyone). You are at one with nature and allowing it to serve as a vehicle for you to travel over the water using just the energy of the water and the movement of the waves.

Skiing and snowboarding rely on gravity alone. With surfing the waves are in harmony with gravity and the contours of the ocean floor and the dynamics of the ocean cause the waves to form and break the way they do. Nature changes the waves constantly with the changing of the tides, the changing wind strength which alters the waves from hour to hour, day to day and year to year. Sometimes new surfing places appear where there weren't waves before because something changed with the contour of the ocean floor. Or once every 10 or 20 years a place cranks up because the conditions are just right, the swells are large enough and heading in the right direction. Technology is so advanced now that they can determine where large swells will occur and a team of big wave surfers converge on the location for a once in a lifetime chance to ride some amazing waves. They also usually bring a film crew, helicopter, jet skis, etc. Well maybe some surfing can be expensive. So I'll just stick to the shore where I can drive to the waves.

With all that being said it comes down do the fact that surfing is an attitude and a state of mind, not just the act of surfing. Once you are a surfer, you'll always be a surfer. The qualities you have that endear you to call yourself a surfer never leaves you. You have respect for the environment, the ocean, the animals, and fish that live in and around the ocean and the beauty of the sea and the seashore. You are a surfer for life, you're stoked and that is a wonderful thing.

California Calling—Beach Boys

If everybody in the U.S.A
Could come with us to Californ-i-a
We could take 'em to a place out west
Where the good sun shines everyday

California callin'
I'll be there right away
There's some beautiful women
Gonna find me one
To show me how to ride the ultimate wave

Now I've joined the surfin' nation and so
I'll take a permanent vacation and go
To the golden shores of 'Frisco Bay
I'll ride 'em all the way to Malibu

And I'll take ya' boogie boardin' with me
'Cause when we're surfin' it's so great to be free
And when you're on a California beach
You might even find 'em windsurfin' too

In the fifties it was "Hey Daddy O"
Then came the surfers and the Hodads ya' know
We had our Woodys and our custom cars
And when we drove around we knew we were bad

My baby listens to my car radio
And when we're cruisin' lets the whole world know
And when our favorite surfin' song comes on
We always let 'em know it's "Totally Rad!" . . .

SURFING ADVENTURES
of the '60s, '70s and beyond . . .

The Old Man Wonders

He can feel the salt spray upon his face
The water is deep and blue
He's relaxed here in his quiet place
Thinking of the days he was surfing the ocean blue

He's old and grey and weather worn
His hands are dry and rough
For the hour is near he'll soon be born
To the sea and the morning duff

He's squeezed his life to the water's edge
But still he continues on
Walking slowly to look over the ledge
And remembers surfing in the early dawn

He wonders how it would be
To be surfing again
The thought alone is aching in him
But it passes with his hopes and fears
The tide comes in
The tide goes out lost and gone
The young surfers ride the waves again
And they're saying life goes on

Andy, 2/11/1970

Surfing Etiquette

photograph by Steve Wilkings

Who's wave it is, right of way?
Keith Paull and Russel Hughes, Hermosa Beach, 1970

There are certain unwritten rules when surfing that "most" surfers abide by. Not all surfers follow the rules though because they haven't learned them yet or they choose to ignore them. This is not the definitive list but it covers most of it, I believe.

1. When paddling out into a wave, stay out of the way of the surfing line of someone riding the wave. When you paddle out, make sure you are out of the way of anyone who might be on a wave.
2. When more than one person is on a wave, the person closest to the curl has the right of the wave. In other words, it is their wave. The person in front should kick out and let the other person ride it out, if possible. But don't drop in behind someone either, if they are already committed to the wave.
3. When you join a group of surfers already surfing a wave set have respect for the lineup situation and don't cut in. Wait for your turn.

SURFING ADVENTURES
of the '60s, '70s and beyond . . .

4. If there are two of you on a wave and neither of you can get out, ride it in as safely as possible without colliding.
5. When checking out unfamiliar locations, respect the locals and other surfers already out there. Pick a spot that works for your ability and the type of surfing you're looking for.
6. In a really crowded set of waves, be courteous, don't bully others, wait for a wave that you can ride safely or go to another spot. In other words, wait for your turn in the lineup; don't crowd in ahead of others.
7. If someone's leash is tangled or snagged, help get it untangled. If someone is in trouble, help them any way you can. In the old days, surfers didn't have leashes so if a surfer lost his board in heavy waves and you were nearby, you would retrieve it for him. And he would do the same for you. If he was closer than the board, you would let him grab onto your board and then paddle over to his board.
8. Take care of your surfboard, wet suit, surf racks, and other equipment. Don't let your equipment get shabby.
9. Always help out the chic surfers, you never know, she may end up taking a liking to you and you could end up surfing into the sunset together. But don't steal another guys surfer girl, that is bad surfing etiquette.
10. Have fun surfing, enjoy yourself, be friendly, meet new people, offer friendly help, or advise to the younger or less experienced surfers. Don't be afraid to talk to a pro or others who are more experienced than you and ask for advice.

***Noble Surfer**—Beach Boys*

The surfers call him "Noble"
And that's just what he is
He's dedicated to the mighty sea

Surfin' night and day
Never twice in one spot
He's somethin' you and I would like to be

Noble (ain't joshin')
Surfer (ain't joshin')
He's the number one man (he's movin')

He's not afraid of body whop
From ten feet or more
He never backs away from a swell

Huaraches on his feet
Bushy hair on his head
And where he's going he'd never tell

A surfin' Cassanova
With his customized board
A Woody and his dirty white jeans . . .

SURFING ADVENTURES
of the '60s, '70s and beyond...

Highway 1 Junction 10

The wide blue oceans with their rolling waves
Paint a picture, against the sky
The wind creates the waves of life
Where all is moving and oceans are alive

Here on the beach I gaze upon
The picture and the holy surfing ground
For all the waves appear the same
And all the surfers have a common frame

The roads of travel for surfers are long and narrow
The valley of rest is the hope of tomorrow
Rivers and streams, canals and lakes
Lead to the ocean, the largest of lakes

In the end one road, one path is left
A river, a stream, the ocean's surf
In the end a mountain, a valley, the sea
That lead to Highway 1 Junction 10, the surfers dream

Andy, 11/13/1969

6

drawing by Ashley Forsyth

Types of Surfers

    Back in the 60s, we kind of put surfers in four categories. I don't think anyone sat down and said these are the types of surfers but it was just something we observed about surfers in general. There were locals, groupers, loners, and competitors.

    Competitors would surf in contests for trophies or prize money. None of us were good enough to get into contests except for Sefo. We mostly just surfed for the enjoyment of surfing. Now maybe we could have competed and maybe some of us could have done fairly well, especially Sefo, because I've seen the contests and didn't think they were all that good but most of them were hotdoggers and did lots of tricks and fancy stuff and that's not what we wanted to get into.

    The loners or what you'd call soul surfers for the most part just kept to themselves and didn't surf with others. Sure there were people around when they surfed but mostly they preferred to surf alone. Now I've surfed by myself but I preferred surfing with a group of my friends.

SURFING ADVENTURES
of the '60s, '70s and beyond . . .

The locals were just that, local surfers that surfed in their "local" spots that they liked to surf, but would venture out to other places occasionally as well.

The groupers, I think, had a lot more fun. It was usually a tight-knit group of guys and sometimes girls that liked to go to the beach together to surf or just hang out. They usually stuck to three or four places that they liked to go. We had about five or six guys in our group but not everyone could make it every time and a couple other guys would join us sometimes or others would come along who were friends but didn't surf, but occasionally they'd give it a try.

Backwards surfing, heels over the end. Unknown Surfer, Hermosa Beach, 1966

Surfing tandem. Tandem Surfing, Carlsbad Contest, 1965

Riding high, trying to keep balanced. David Nuuhiwa, Huntington Beach Contest, 1966

Spectators watching a surf contest. Carlsbad Surf Contest, 1966
photograph by Steve Wilkings

Surfer Joe—The Surfaris

Down in Dohenee Where the surfers all go
There's a big beach blonde named Surfer Joe
He's got a green surfboard
With a Woody to match
And when he rides the freeway
Man is he hard to catch

Surfer Joe, now look at him go
Surfer surfer surfer Joe
Go man go surfer Joe

He went down to Huntington Beach one week
For the annual surfers convention meet
He was hangin' five and walkin' the nose
And when the meet was over the trophy was Joe's

Surfer Joe, now look at him go
Surfer surfer surfer Joe
Go man go surfer Joe . . .

Then there were these guys called nomads who weren't really surfers at all, they just liked to carry around a surfboard on their car all the time even though they never went surfing. A friend of mine was like that. He had an orange VW bug and when I saw him with his VW bug, he always was carrying two surfboards. So I figured he was a pretty good surfer but he didn't really seem like the surfer type to me. One day I asked him if he'd like to go to the beach and he agreed and I put my board on his rack and we headed to San Clemente. When we got there, we took the boards off but he only took one; he left the 8'6" Hobbie on the rack. When we got down to the beach, I started waxing my board but Charlie said he was gonna wait awhile. I surfed for a couple of hours and never saw him come out. He claimed he was surfing down the beach a little so after I rested awhile, I tried to get him to go out again. This time I kept a close eye on him to see if he'd come in. He actually came in but all he did was ride in the white water on his belly. I guess he hadn't gotten the hang of it yet. On the way home, I asked about his 8'6" Hobbie that he didn't use and he said he was thinking about selling it. So I

SURFING ADVENTURES
of the '60s, '70s and beyond . . .

asked him how much he was asking for it. He said $20 so I told him I'd see if my brother, Chris, wanted it because he was thinking about trying to learn to surf. After talking to Chris, he said he'd like to get it but only had $10 so I told him we'll go 50/50 and I could use it whenever I wanted to borrow it. He agreed and I think I ended up using it more than he did. He tried it once at Leo Carillo when we were on vacation. I don't know if he ever stood up for more than a second or two, but at least he tried. I asked him recently and he told me that it was right that he only stood up for a couple of seconds just that one time. I ended up buying it from him outright not long after that. I used it a few times but it was a lot wider than the Royal Hawaiian and a little harder to maneuver so I seldom used it unless I had a ding in my board that was under repair. I couldn't use the 7' board on waves over six because it was too difficult to get up the speed needed to catch those waves.

I never went with Charlie again but we still hung out sometimes. I never asked him about his surfing as I knew he hadn't been out surfing because he didn't have a tan. Charlie was an okay guy, just kind of a loner and nomad.

Instrumental: The Lonely Surfer—Jack Nitzsche

Today's Surfer types

Nowadays, you would categorize surfers in a lot more categories based on the types of waves they like, the style of surfing, or size of the waves. As a kid, we used to take a piece of round wood or plastic and use it as a skim board and slide it along on two to three inches of water along the shore and jump on it and see how far we could skim along the water; sometimes we'd hit it wrong and land on our butt and other times we'd stop dead in the sand and land on our nose and get a mouthful of sand. People must have gotten a good laugh watching us but somebody else must have taken notice because next year, we saw skim boards for sale in the beach shops. Some with Styrofoam under the board and some nicely made ones that would hold up for a long time. Today they've taken skim boarding to a whole new level. I've seen them on TV where they start off on the skim water but then take off into the shore break waves, do aerials, or even turn right into the waves for a little ride.

There's also boogie boarding, belly boarding, or knee boarding, which have been around a long time as well as bodysurfing. Some of the better bodysurfers use fins and can do some amazing things. I've even seen some boogie boarders stand up on their board, especially amazing was the guy riding at the Wedge, standing up on six- to eight-foot waves with nothing but a foot of water below him. That guy was amazing.

This probably isn't what I'd call the definitive list of the types of surfers but you'll get the idea. You have the first Big Wave surfers of Waimea: Greg Noll, Mickey Munoz, Mike Stang, Pat Curren, Bob Bermel, Bing Copeland, and Del Cannon. Even Giant Wave surfers like Laird Hamilton, Ken Bradshaw, Jeff Clark, Evan Slater, Buzzy Kerbox, Darrick Doerner, Mike Parsons, Brad Gerlach, Kenny Collins, Peter Mel, and others—who ride some really big waves of 30-70' plus by being towed in with a wave runner or jet ski—sometimes they use a hydrofoil to actually lift the board above the water to be able to glide on the wave. You have professional surfing contests with some really good prize money now. Specialty surfers, tube surfers, aerial surfers, hot dogging, or trick surfers, you still have the soul surfers, loners, groupers, and locals. There are small wave riders, short board and long board riders. In the old days, during the 60s, you even saw tandem surfers, usually a guy and a girl on an extra long board. Today you don't see tandem surfing as much except maybe in Hawaii. In the 60s, they used long boards of ten feet plus called "guns" to help them catch the big waves. Now with tow-in surfing, they use a short 5-6' foot board with straps similar to what wake boarders use. The guys that use the hydrofoil actually use snowboard boots loosely fitted so they can slip out easily. There are windsurfers, which you can even do without waves, even on a lake or river with a nice breeze. On the open ocean, some people windsurf between the islands in Hawaii getting up to 40-50 mph, when the wind is right. There are west coast surfers and east coast surfers (but these are usually smaller waves). There are guys that surf all year around the world searching for big waves. I saw people surfing in Galveston, Texas, when I was there a couple of years ago. Some guys even surf in the Gulf of Mexico riding the wake of ships traveling along the shipping lanes. Some guys surf in the Michigan Lakes when the wind kicks up or in a river where the water backwash is just right and forms a little standing wave that you can ride on. Most surfers like medium-sized waves where you can do some tricks and some hot dogging. You also have beginners who usually are riding the white water, which is very difficult to stand up in. But once you can get up in white water, you can get up easy on the face of the wave. Of course there are kids who are learning to surf and are the future of the sport. And now there some people doing kite surfing, parasail surfing, or kayak surfing; did

SURFING ADVENTURES
of the '60s, '70s and beyond . . .

I mention windsurfing? There are still guys that are local surfers that pretty much just stay near where they can easily drive to and then there are the guys who travel all over the world using hi-tech equipment searching for giant waves, filming their rides, and making movies for us to watch and be envious and realize that we'd get killed if we tried what they are doing. Some of the waves they get are absolutely incredible like the one Laird rode at Teaupoo, Tahiti, in August 2001.

There are old time surfers, guys who've been around forever who are still able to get out there and enjoy surfing. I ran into a guy a Seal Beach in March 2008 surfing and he said he had been surfing since 1960—48 years—and he looked to be in pretty good shape. And you've got kids out there learning the sport and, in fact, they are the future of the sport. And of course the girls and women have always been out there surfing and they, too, fit in all those categories. Today there is a lot more exposure, competitions, and magazines about surfing. The ladies, too, have been getting a lot more press and are being included in films, which is good for the sport. There have been a few Hollywood movies about surfing in the last ten to fifteen years as well which helps the sport also. And, of course, the guys and gals who surf in Hawaii at Waikiki, the North Shore, and the outer islands and reefs. Most surfers fall into more than one of these categories. In the 50s, surfers were often thought of as surf bums because they were misunderstood. They were mostly free spirits who enjoyed doing something different from the normal. And that's what surfing is really all about—being a free spirit, enjoying life, and doing something that a lot of people are not able to do. And then telling stories, in movies or books, about their adventures for future generations to enjoy.

painting by Garry Birdsall

Worth the Drive

Nowhere in Particular

It's time to go surfing no where in particular
    we'll take a sailboat to get there
And then we'll surf until we need to move on
    or until we have nowhere in particular to go

Our last surfing trip
    was about a year ago
It was nowhere in particular
    we surfed and played all day
Then we stayed a little longer
    surfing until sunset everyday

Where do you want to go?
    nowhere in particular
What do you want to do?
    nothing in particular
How are we gonna get there?
    not really sure, I'm not too particular
I don't know but we'll have some fun!
    Somewhere—but nowhere in particular

Let's go on a sailboat
    maybe we'll charter a fishing boat
We could fly to St. Somewhere
    or hitch a ride on an ocean freighter
To surf nowhere in particular would do
    As long as I'm with you

Surfing on a tropical island sounds just fine
    somewhere in the middle of the ocean
It could be in the South Pacific
    or the Hawaiian Islands, I really don't mind
We'll surf all day in the sun
    until the wind begs us to move on
In fact surfing nowhere in particular
    is right where I want to be

Andy, 12/20/2005

SURFING ADVENTURES
of the '60s, '70s and beyond...

Smooth ride. Ken Rocky, K-38 Mexico, 1966

A little crowded but not too bad. Dana Point, 1964

photographs by Steve Wilkings

7

painting by Bruno Turpin

How Old Do You Have To Be?

(Spring of 1970)

    During spring break, most kids head off to the beaches or the Colorado River for a week of craziness, partying, and drinking. At the river, people would go water skiing or boating, and at the beach, well they did everything you do at those other places including surfing. In the east, kids head down to Florida, like Ft. Lauderdale, Palm Beach, Daytona, or some of the other hot spots to get an early jump on summer.
    In the spring of 1970, Dan and I decided to go to Mexico for spring break this year. We were gonna stop in San Diego on the first day and go to the San Diego Zoo. Then make our way down to Tijuana and then Encenada. I had never been to Encenada but I heard that there was some

good surfing down there. Dan didn't surf but I had met him in my senior year of high school. He had grown up in Japan because his dad was a US diplomat and he went to the schools there. He spoke fluent Japanese and considered it his main language. He wrote some poems in Japanese and taught me a few words. He was technically a junior but at the end of his junior year, he only needed one history class to graduate and wanted to start college in the fall instead of waiting until the next quarter. I told him of an adult night school nearby that my mom had gone to. He checked it out and he signed up for the class and was able to get his high school diploma and got accepted into college that fall. We both attended California State Polytechnic College in Pomona, California, or Cal Poly Pomona. There is also a Cal Poly, San Luis Obispo, farther north. A few years later the "College" was changed to "University."

We got an early start and we arrived around 10:00 AM in San Diego and headed over to the San Diego Zoo. I think it was $7 to get in, which was a lot back then. Now it's something like $35 or $40. It was a nice day, plenty of sunshine, just a slight breeze. The animals were great to see. We basically just walked all around the zoo checking out the animals and also the girls. There weren't a lot of girls but we did manage to talk to some girls who happened to be on spring break too and were attending San Diego State University. We told them where we were going and after a few minutes, we said goodbye. We offered to take them with us but we didn't think they'd really go along but it was worth asking.

By about 4:00 PM, we decided we should get going and left the zoo to go to Tijuana for about an hour and then on to Encenada, hoping to get there before it got dark. It was only about fifty miles so we figured we had plenty of time. Well we didn't get far when the car started to sound funny, almost like a flat tire. It only made the noise between about 10-25 mph. When I went faster like 35 mph, it was okay. But I was concerned so we found a service station that could also make repairs. The mechanic was leaving by 5:00 PM but he said he'd check it out real quick. He thought it was probably a bearing in the axle and he could fix it in the morning and should only take a couple of hours. So we were stuck for the evening. We made the best of it and decided to get some dinner at a nearby Denny's and then go see a movie, if we could find a theatre. Turns out there was one just around the corner a couple of blocks away. I don't remember what we saw but it was good to relax for a while. After the movie, we went back to the car and sacked out for the night.

We used to sleep in the car sometimes to save money. But actually, it was out of necessity because we didn't have enough money for a room. My dad gave me his credit card in case the car had trouble or for other emergencies. The next morning, we talked to the mechanic and he said they'd have it fixed in a couple of hours, which was great. So we walked over to the nearby Denny's and got some breakfast. I called my dad to let him know what was going on with the car and that I'd have to use the credit card and that it was going to be around $25 to repair it. My car was nicknamed the "Blue Burrito." It was a 59 Ford Galaxy 500 4-door with a 292 cc, 8-cylinder engine. It was aqua-green-blue with a white top. I could get my 7' surfboard inside normally but on this trip, I brought along my Royal Hawaiian 9'2" board and so we put both boards on the racks. After we had finished breakfast, we went over to check on the car and they had it ready. It was only $25 for the new bearing and labor.

Well by about 10:00 AM, we were on our way again. It was just a short time and we were at the border of Mexico and about to enter Tijuana. They usually stop you to find out where you're going and how long you're going to stay. We told them Tijuana for the day and then on to Encenada to do some surfing and sightseeing. I guess we didn't look like crooks or criminals and we did have the surfboards so they let us pass.

We stopped in Tijuana and looked around the shops and I picked up a few things. I got a brown suede leather jacket with long frills for $17.50. Originally they wanted $25 but they like to barter so I talked him down some. We came to Tijuana a couple of times when we were kids and got to see how to barter with the salespeople by watching our parents. I took Spanish in high school so I could talk with them a little. They probably were laughing at my poor Spanish but it really didn't matter as long as I got a good deal. I also picked up a brown leather floppy hat for a couple bucks, a souvenir Bowie style knife with a hand-carved Indian Head handle for a couple bucks, and a 12-string guitar for about $25 dollars, which they wanted $60 for. I later sold it for $35 at a swap meet about a year later. They used to have swap meets every Saturday and Sunday during the day at the old drive-in movie theatres.

Dan got some things too but I don't remember exactly what he got, but I think he may have gotten a jacket. After a couple of hours, we headed out and were on our way or so we thought. As we were heading for the highway to Encenada, we saw a truck driving along with the tires wobbling a lot. We noticed that of the seven lug nuts it was supposed to have on the left front tire, it only had two lug nuts and the rear had only three and none of them were fastened that tightly. It looked like the tires would fall off any minute. It was a pretty large truck and was carrying a lot of junk, mostly heavy metal parts of some kind.

We made it by safely and after a few blocks, we were just about to the highway. It seemed like my car fit right in with all the other cars in Tijuana because there were a lot of 59 Fords, Aqua-Green with a white top. Just as we were about to approach the highway entrance, there were two European looking girls hitchhiking with backpacks. They were definitely not Mexican but looked to be French or Italian but we drove by without stopping. We looked in the rearview mirror and they threw up their arms apparently hoping for a ride. So we stopped, talked about it a minute, and decided to go back and see where they were going. Our backseat was kind of full but since I had a big car, we would have enough room for all four of us in the front. So we went back to talk to them. It turns out that they were French art students in college and were traveling around North America and doing drawings and paintings as part of a class project. They were hoping to get to Encenada so we offered them a ride and they put their backpacks in the back and hopped in. It was a little tight with four in the front but they didn't seem to mind. They spoke a little English and told us about being from France and that they were art students in college. They have been traveling the US and Canada for three months and were just now making it into Mexico. They would be traveling until near the end of the summer. Now these young ladies were from Europe and France in particular; I had never met anyone from Europe. I knew they didn't bathe as often as we do and these young ladies hadn't bathed apparently in quite some time. So leaving the windows open was definitely a necessity.

They showed us some of their sketches and they were quite good. As we were driving, I think they were sketching us because after we got to Encenado, we wanted to see what they were sketching but they wouldn't show us. I figured out later that they were sketching instead of using a camera. I guess that was a good way for them to appreciate things and improve their artistic skills. We stopped near a trailer park. The young ladies thanked us for the ride and headed out. They said they'd be back later but they never did come back. We didn't even have a chance to offer to take them to dinner; they just took off. I guess they were on a mission.

We decided to walk around the trailer park to see what it was like and were kind of hoping to run into the girls but never saw them. There was a rec room there with a grill. The rec room had a couple of pool tables, pinball machine, ping-pong table, and a foosball game. We got some food then played a little pool. Our college had some foosball games and we used to play against some of the hustlers who liked to bet on games but I wouldn't bet because I didn't want to lose my money and I wasn't that good, but I enjoyed playing and did get pretty good after awhile. I was better at pool and the only time I ever bet on pool, I ended up winning $3.

The trailer park had a generator running to keep the lights going but they would give out about every twenty to thirty minutes for a short time until they got them started again. After a few games of pool, foosball, ping-pong, and pinball, we asked if there was a place we could buy some beer. They told us we had to go into town so we drove back to town about two miles. We found a liquor store and picked up a couple six-packs of Dos Equis and some rocket firecrackers and some other small fireworks and a lighter. The drinking age in California was 21 and so we didn't know what the age was in Mexico for buying beer. I was only 19 and I had the beer and since I didn't want to risk using my poor Spanish, I asked,

"How old to you have to be to buy a six-pack of beer?"

Maybe he didn't understand English that well but he knew I was speaking English because he answered me.

"A dolla ninety eight ($1.98)."

So we gave him the money for two six-packs, chips, fireworks, and lighter and went on our way. So now we know how old you have to be to buy beer in Mexico, $1.98. We were in hysterics and would tell that story at every party. In fact I still tell that story whenever I get the chance—which is one of the stories that inspired me to write this book.

That evening, after drinking a couple of beers, we used the empty bottles as rocket launchers and sat on the cliffs shooting off the rocket firecrackers over the ocean. We had a lot of fun and after a while, we finished off the beer and crashed in the car. We had to move some things around so Dan could get in the backseat, and put some stuff in the trunk.

The next day, I got up early to head down to the water to catch some waves. The waves were breaking fast off the point about 5-8' with a nice left shoulder, perfect for my goofy foot stance. I surfed for about four to five hours until the wind started changing directions and messed up the waves and made them too choppy.

SURFING ADVENTURES
of the '60s, '70s and beyond...

Catch A Wave—Beach Boys

Catch a wave and you're sittin' on top of the world

Don't be afraid to try the greatest sport around
Catch a wave, catch a wave
Those who don't just have to put it down
You paddle out turn around and raise
And baby, that's all there is to the coastline craze

You gotta
Catch a wave and you're sittin' on top of the world

Not just a fad cause it's been going on so long
Catch a wave, catch a wave
They say it wouldn't last too long
They'll eat their words with a fork and spoon
They'll hit the road and I'll be surfin' soon

When they
Catch a wave and you're sittin' on top of the world...

    Since we lost a day because of the car breaking down, we decided to head back to San Diego and do some surfing there. I needed to get gas and when we got to a gas station, they were selling it by the liter. We figured out later that it was about 25 cents a gallon. We were paying around 29 cents a gallon in 1970.
    We decided to take the main highway which was a toll road and it cost like 25 cents for three tolls along the way. It was a nice road with almost no cars on it. When we got back to the border, we had to declare anything we bought. So I told them about the jackets and hat and the guitar. They thought I said car and I had to say, "no no, a guitar," and show them. They said okay. Then I told them about the knife and they wanted to see it. They took it over to the supervisor to see and they passed it around to everyone and then we finally got it back. We figured we got it back only because on the sheath it had stamped "Souvenir of Mexico" and it had an Indian Head on the handle.

After we finally made it across the border, we stopped into San Diego and hit a couple of the beaches and I did some surfing. Then after an hour or so, we went on up to Cardiff-by-the-Sea for the rest of the day. We first stopped at Edmund's house to see if he'd let us stay on his lot and he remembered me and said it was okay by him. So after I did some surfing there, we got some food and crashed on his lot. But we checked around for dry spots, if you know what I mean. We got our sleeping bags and slept pretty good.

The next day, I got in some more surfing and then we headed home in the afternoon. What a great time we had, got in a lot of surfing in a new place, and we knew that in a couple of days, we'd have to get back to the routine of classes again. What a drag. But most importantly, we now know that in order to buy a six-pack of beer in Mexico you have to be a $1.98.

A Beautiful Memory

The memory book I treasure
Is bringing happy thoughts to me
Oh! It's been nearly two years ago
Since I left my friends in Japan

I remember a good-bye party
Their friendly faces float in my mind
It was even hard to say good-bye
To a girl I had just met

A song was sung
By a poet friend
That told of me
Leaving Japan

If I could only re-live that last year
That gave me the happiest times of my life
I wish that my friends were near
But how long till that day will come

Dan Brown, 2/25/1970

8

photograph by Andy Forsyth

Flat Waves, Fog, and Rainy Days

Flat Days

Not every day is a perfect sunny day for surfing. Sometimes the waves are just plain flat. That's really a bummer especially if it is a nice day. All you can do is to make the most of it. You could do some skim boarding, skateboarding, or you can find a pickup game of volleyball, toss around a Frisbee, or play football—if you can get a bunch of guys together. Beach football is great. Mainly because when you fall in the sand it doesn't hurt and it really gives your legs a good workout. Some people seem to run better in the sand than others do.

Instrumental: Walk Don't Run—The Ventures

Surfin' in the Fog

The weirdest thing is surfing when it is foggy. I guess because you're used to having the sunshine, but it's still pretty cool. The toughest part though is reading the waves coming in because you can't see them until they are almost on you. Sort of like night surfing with a full moon. But at least with a full moon, you can see the waves forming. Now if you've ever tried surfing at night without the moon, then that is really tough because there is no light to help you see the waves.

And in the Rain

Rainy days are almost like foggy days because there isn't a lot of light and visibility is low. The good part is because you're in the water anyway and you're going to get wet, so it doesn't really matter. The bad part is you're not going to be able to dry off and get warm.

SURFING ADVENTURES
of the '60s, '70s and beyond...

The Sun Never Came Up—Scott Kirby
www.scottkirby.com

Heard some bad news on the tube last night
While sitting at the hotel bar
Took a deep breath and finished my tequila
And went out to look at the stars
Dawn seemed to come with a struggle
As I walked the six miles to the beach
I sat myself down on the old sea wall
To try to learn what the sea could teach

And the sun never came up, and the surf never came in,
An old beach bum on an old beach blanket said, I'll never surf again,
And the girl from California, With her life in the shopping cart
Sang "God Only Knows" to her transistor radio, and rolled off in the dark

I sat there waiting for the tide to turn
But this day the water lay low
The big gray ocean lat flat and still
No warmth of the sun, no ebb and flow
And the boys with their boards in the pickup trucks
Looked around and said man what goes
The beach bum said, boys there's no surfin
All the beaches are closed

The boys put their boards in the pickup truck
And drove off in the rain
The old beach bum packed his old beach blanket
And shuffled off to catch the train
And the girl from California
With her life in the shopping cart
Sang God only knows to her transistor radio
And rolled off in the dark

And the sun never came up, and the surf never came in,
An old beach bum on an old beach blanket said, I'll never surf again,
And the girl from California, With her life in the shopping cart
Sang "God Only Knows" to her transistor radio, and rolled off in the dark

Raindrops of Life

Spacious are the waters of the sea.
Fresh air flows over the tide waters,
And heaven lets itself be known.

Raining down on the earth
Churning up the waves
With it's mighty wind

A year has gone by
Since I was living a surfer's dream
Like the waters flowing down stream.

When the rain falls on the ground,
The water flows into the ocean,
I can't help but think of this as—

All the people in the world.
Being as small drops of rain
Flowing down their own path of life.

Until one day they are washed to sea.
To the great ocean of humanity.
Then, like all the others.

With no way to retreat.
This little rain drop,
Is at home in the waves of the ocean.

Andy, 10/3/1972

Ashes Falling

The other weird surfing day was when there were the ten thousand wildfires and the clouds of smoke were dropping ashes and the sun coming through the smoke clouds made the water look red and ashes were falling on the water, the surfboard, and you. Now that was really an eerie feeling. I will talk about this more in another chapter.

Heart of a Beach Town—Scott Kirby

Empty beaches just a boy and his dog
Ice blue water breaks on snow covered rocks
Old man winter you ain't getting me down
Cause this is the heart, this is the heart
This is the heart, this is the heart, of a beach town

This old house is moaning
And this old house is groaning
As the night wind roars with a rage
And that perfect storm passes
And the sun comes out
And the boys are out catching their waves

http://www.scottkirby.com/

Big Waves, Cold Water

painting by Bruno Turpin

Waimea Drop

In the winter, the waves can get bigger because of the storms that form off the coast of Mexico or farther up the coast; but the water is colder too. You can still surf but you'll most likely need a wet suit. Your fingers, and toes get numb and turn blue, and your brain can get that ice cream freeze. By the time your fingers are numb, you can't feel how cold it is anyway and then you're okay, except that you could get hyperthermia, which we didn't know about back then, we just knew, IT WAS FREAKING COLD! Winter surfing is what proves that you're really addicted to surfing to be able to put up with these conditions just to ride the bigger waves. Now if you were in Hawaii during the winter surfing, you could get the big waves and still have the warmer temperatures. But in Alaska or Washington State, it's cold all the time.

SURFING ADVENTURES
of the '60s, '70s and beyond . . .

Ride the Wild Surf—Jan and Dean

In Hawaii there's place known as Waimea Bay
Where the best surfers in the world come to stay
To ride the wild surf they come to try
To conquer those waves some thirty feet high

Ride ride ride the wild surf
Ride ride ride the wild surf
Ride ride ride the wild surf
Gotta take that one last ride

Surf fever brings 'em here to meet the test
And hanging round the beach you'll see the best
They're waxed up and ready just a waiting for
The set to build up on the Northern Shore

Ride ride ride the wild surf
Ride ride ride the wild surf
Ride ride ride the wild surf
Gotta take that one last ride . . .

Grey Suits

Internet open source

Shark looking for lunch, I'd get out of there pronto.

The biggest bummer is coming upon a great surfing spot, nice weather, waves breaking just right, and seeing those grey suits swimming in circles in the water. You know you can't go out because you don't want to be their breakfast or lunch. But sometimes, you get there first and the sharks show up a little later after you've been there awhile and then you have to make a quick exit before you get a bite taken out of you. When you are in a new area that you've never been in before, you're always on the lookout for the "fins." But dolphin fins are good because they keep the sharks away. Otters and seals don't bother you either but sometimes they like to play with you and have fun themselves by bodysurfing or teasing you, especially the otters.

Whale of a Good Time

Humpback whales in the waters of Southern California are a real treat and lots of boats go out when they are migrating. Occasionally a whale gets beached, which is really unfortunate. I remember one time a small whale was beached at San Clemente. They had the whole area roped off because it must have grounded overnight and had already died. I don't remember for sure what type of whale it was but it made the TV news that night and all the newspaper headlines.

Not long ago, a couple of whales got into the Sacramento River and they had to work to get them turned around so that they could get back out to sea.

Sea World in San Diego had a humpback whale and also several killer whales that were trained to do tricks. It was always fun to go to Sea World and see those shows. I got to see a show when I was in Hawaii in 1973 at Sea World where the trainers were riding on the back of a killer whale. I never got to see a whale in the ocean but I hope to someday. This coming August, 2008, I'm planning on going on a cruise in Alaska with my family and fiancée. We're planning on going on a whale watching excursion while we are on the cruise. My parents used to have a sailboat in Dana Point, California, and have told me that they have seen whales on occasion.

SURFING ADVENTURES
of the '60s, '70s and beyond...

Whales are such an awesome creature and one of the last remaining species left from prehistoric times along with the Great White Shark and some others. It is such a blessing that we have these creatures and a tragedy that they were on the brink of extinction. Hopefully that will never happen due to our own ignorance and greed.

Tennis Shoes

At Leo Carrillo State Beach walking out through the rocks can be a challenge so we decided to try surfing with tennis shoes on. It was different but you didn't need to put wax on the board. That was good and bad. Good because when you were paddling out on your stomach the wax didn't chafe your stomach and chest. Not everyone can knee paddle, which is very rough on your knees because you get surfing knobs. I was born with mini-surfing knobs so when I tried knee paddling it hurt way too much so I just stuck with stomach paddling. The bad part about being on your stomach is that you don't have as good a look at the waves because you're lower in the water. The bad part about not putting wax on your board is you don't have anything to keep you from sliding off the board, so we put some wax on anyway.

Changes in the Wind

Sometimes just the change in the tide or wind can affect the waves and they don't break right anymore or the wind will shift and the waves will become choppy or close out too fast or the wind is strong enough blowing offshore that the waves hang up and break too close to shore. One night when the tide was high and the wind was blowing out to sea the waves were crashing right on the shore at Huntington around 10-12'. Since we were that close to the waves it sounded like a cannon going off it was that loud. At the time it was the biggest shore break I'd ever seen.

painting by Garry Birdsall

Holden Ute'

The Grunion are Running

When there is a full moon, which is also very high tide, during the summer the grunion can be out. It is called grunion running. These are little fish that look like sardines. And thousands or maybe even tens of thousands are washed up on the beach. They are partially digging themselves in the sand laying their eggs, and then the males come in behind them and dig in with the females and fertilize the eggs. We used to get buckets and pick up some to use as fish bait or to cook and eat. I've only seen this happen about three times but I believe that it only happens during the summer. It lasts for a couple hours then they go back out to sea. This only occurs during a full moon, probably so the males can see the females better. I wonder if they have to buy them a drink first?

Dune Buggy

Just south of San Louis Obispo at the Oceano Dunes State Vehicular Recreational Area we used to ride a jeep or dune buggy around on the Sand Dunes. When we got tired of that we'd climb to the top of the

SURFING ADVENTURES
of the '60s, '70s and beyond . . .

dunes with our surf boards and ride down the dunes standing on our boards. We'd take the fins off and glide down or ride the board backwards with the fin up a little if it wouldn't come off. It was a lot of fun but not as much fun as snow surfing down the toboggan trails in the winter up in the mountains. Now that was really cool and cold too.

Surf Movies

If you didn't get enough surfing during the day you could always go see a surfing movie at night. These were usually near the beach at a school, old theatre or sometimes a regular theatre. The cost was usually pretty reasonable like 10 cents or 25 cents depending on how long it was.

And the Waves

The West Coast skies seldom rain in the summer
And the shores are sunny, hot, and dry
The water never warmer
Than the sand and the sky
And the waves are given to the surfers

The seagulls roam the empty beaches
In the morning when people aren't there
But when people come to the beaches
The seagulls cannot stay anywhere
And the waves are carrying the surfers

When the sun scorches the sand
People are getting tan or burned
While songs are playing on the radio
As people sing with the band
And the waves are larger than the people

The people now are leaving the beaches
Seagulls again play in the sand
The sun is falling into the ocean
As quiet descends on the land
And the waves are losing the surfers

The moon is bright while the air is warm
Fires light the beaches aglow
A whisper of music echoes around
While the seagulls fly low
And the waves are missing the surfers

Andy, 4/18/1995

9

photograph by Jane Forsyth

Hot Dogs and Marshmallows

Sometimes going to the beach wasn't always about going surfing but just hanging out with your friends. Our youth group at church every year would go to the beach for a day trip beach party. We always went to Huntington State Beach or Corona del Mar because of all the fire rings. I first went on one of these trips when I was younger because my dad was driving the truck. The church would rent a truck that would hold about thirty kids in the back and a few others drove separately and were able to bring all the food, drinks, and music. They'd bring coolers with soft drinks, chips, ice, hot dogs, all the fixings, marshmallows, and firewood.

We'd get there early around 10:00-11:00 AM, and they'd stake out a couple of good fire rings and then they'd head on down to the beach. They'd usually get a football game going or set up for beach volleyball or some people would get in the water for swimming, bodysurfing, and hanging out by the water. Others would just like to lie around soaking up the rays or building sand castles. As a kid I usually liked to help with the sand castles, look for seashells, or play in the surf.

After a long day of activities, they would break out the record players for some beach music and dancing in the sand. It always seemed like a lot of fun. As I got older, I would get more involved with the activities. The last couple of years, we couldn't use the trucks anymore because of the insurance risks so we all had to go in cars. It took a lot more coordination and volunteers to drive but we could take more stuff.

One of the guys in our youth group, Tim, brought a surfboard once and he tried to get out and surf but the waves were kind of choppy and he couldn't get past the breakwater. He couldn't go out to surf until after the lifeguards went in which was around 5:00 PM. The waves really weren't that good for surfing but he was determined. We'd watch him go over the falls sideways, holding onto the board for dear life or even go end-over-end one time still holding on. We were laughing so hard because no one really liked him that much but it was just funny watching him getting beat up by the waves. After a few minutes, it was obvious that he had never surfed before because he couldn't get past the first set of breakers to set up. The waves were only about four feet and not well formed. I guess he gave up after awhile but at least he tried. I thought he should have tried the waves closer in but since it was high tide and choppy, the waves weren't very rideable. At that time, I hadn't been surfing a lot yet but knew enough to know what to do to get out and how to catch a wave and what waves might be rideable.

Instrumental: Wipeout—The Surfaris

Hehehehheheee Wipe oooout!

SURFING ADVENTURES
of the '60s, '70s and beyond...

Wipeout—Beach Boys

Heheheheheee Wipe ooooout!

Wipin' out wipe out
Wipin' out wipe out

For three years straight we toured the nation
When we get through we needed a vacation
We wanted to party and get a little rest
So we packed our things and headed out west
We got our surfboards took the beachball out
Jumped in a limousine ready to "Wipeout"

We got to California I said headed for the beach
There were girls galore all within our reach
There was sand and sun and lots of fun
But when we get there the fun really begun
So we cut on the box and started to shout
It was the Beach Boys rockin' huh huh the "Wipeout"

The sun went down and the night began
We was rapping for the people cold chillin' boppin'
We was partying hard making lots of noise
When around the corner came the real Beach Boys
So we all jumped up and started to shout
"Let's all sing the song called the 'Wipeout'" ...

As evening crept in, we'd watch the sun set and by then, people would have started up the fire rings. It was quite a sight to see two rows of fire rings glowing with orange flames as far as the eye could see. Some of them had some pretty big bond fires going, and of course, music playing at nearly every fire ring. Most were cooking hot dogs or hamburgers, chicken, shish kebab, and other great food on the open flames and with all the condiments. There'd always be baked beans in a big pot too. Sometimes we'd dig up a few clams and roast them on the fire; some people liked them. I tried one but it was kind of rubbery. Not my thing, so I guess I'll stick to the hot dogs, hamburgers, beans, chips and the other food. What a great time it was.

Inevitably there was always someone strolling from campfire to campfire with a guitar ready to sing songs for anyone willing to listen and give him something to eat. We always thought of these guys as beach bums because they were kinda grungy. Little did we know then but we do now that these guys were probably homeless.

After a while, we'd start singing campfire songs and then start cooking up the marshmallows. If you didn't have a commercially made hot dog stick, then you'd have to make one with wire coat hangers. You first straightened it out and formed a handle with the hooked part by creating about a 6" handle and wrapping the tightly coiled part around the straight part to make the handle so it wouldn't come apart. Then you'd break off the tip so you'd have a straight end that you could stick the hot dogs and marshmallows into. You'd start working the end of it in and out of the sand about twelve inches for a few minutes to get all the paint or clear coating off of it. Then after the fire was nice and hot, you'd stick it into the fire for a few minutes and then you'd work it in the sand again for a few minutes. Then again back into the fire. You then had to let it cool off and clean it with a paper towel. You were now ready to cook a hot dog. When it was time to eat marshmallows, you'd want to clean it off by again working it in the sand, then put it in the fire, clean it, and then you'd be ready for the marshmallows.

You could pop on a couple of marshmallows and hold them just over the coals, rotating them until they were golden brown. Some people would put them between a couple of graham crackers and chocolate bars to make smores, but I didn't know what they were doing until years later. Most people ate the marshmallows right off the wire or let them flame for a few seconds to get them black and then eat them after they cooled off.

SURFING ADVENTURES
of the '60s, '70s and beyond . . .

Slow Down Summer—Rob Mehl

Sixty-three, junior high,
Waitin' for that pretty little blonde to walk by,
Streamline chassis, twinkle in her eye,
And all I can say is, "my, my, my!"

Beach Boy summer, sixty-five,
Surfin' Stone Steps, great to be alive,
Sneakin' dad's car out for a midnight drive,
Down to Beacon' for a dive, dive.

Slow down, summer, you're gone too fast,
You're the best of times, but you never last.
Slow down, summer, wait for me,
I'm tryin' to grow old gracefully.
Slow down, summer. Slow down, summer.

Remember sixty-seven, nobody else does,
Drivin' with a license, shavin' the peach fuzz,
Laughin' at Waldo with the flat-top buzz,
Doin' what came natural, just because.

Way too soon it was sixty-nine,
Mustang Sally was a good friend of mine,
One more memory for auld lang syne,
So many summers that were fine, fine.

Every now and again as the years go by
I'll think of an old song and sigh, sigh.
Better love what I've got before it's gone,
Can't remember the name of that pretty little blonde.

www.robmehl.com

The trip home was always cold in the back of the truck. So when we couldn't take the big truck anymore, it was better because we were in a warm car for the ride home. In the truck the hour-ride home usually took an hour and a half; it was cold, the tarp covered the back of the truck bed, mostly blocking the wind but it was still cold. On the way home, we'd be talking about all the things we did that day or what happened on previous trips. It was always a great time and we couldn't wait to do it again the next year.

Which Way Does the Wind Blow

Which way does the wind blow
When does the sunset
Where do the seagulls go
Get out the surfboards and let's find out

The wind can change at any time
It can make the waves large or small
The wind can push the waves forward
As you surf the swells

The sun rises in the east
And it sets in the west
In the summer it goes down slowly
In the winter it falls too fast

The seagulls really don't travel far
They stay near the shores
They like to squawk and make some noise
Teasing the surfer gals and guys

When we surf around the world
No matter where we go
We need the wind to make the waves
So the wind it blows for us

SURFING ADVENTURES
of the '60s, '70s and beyond . . .

When we surf around the world
No matter where we go
We see some amazing sunsets
So the sun it sets for us

When we surf around the world
No matter where we go
The seagulls are flying near the shore
So the seagulls are waiting to tease us

When we surf around the world
No matter where we go
The wind and the sunsets and the seagulls
Are always there for us

Andy, 12/20/2005

10

painting by Garry Birdsall

Parties, Girls, Horseback Riding, Bicycling

Sunset on the Beach

There's nothing like being at the beach when you have someone to share it with, like a group of friends, relatives, or just someone special that makes the time even better. A friend of mine, Richard, was at his house in Florida not long after his second divorce and said he was sitting on the beach watching the sun go down. "What's the point of enjoying a beautiful sunset if you don't have anyone to share it with?" How true. It's almost like the saying, "If a tree falls in the forest and no one is around, does it make a noise?"

SURFING ADVENTURES
of the '60s, '70s and beyond . . .

Internet open source

Sunset

I Live for the Sun—*The Sunrays*

Go—Sun Sun Sun Sun
Sun Sun Sun Sun

I live for the Sun
Because it makes fun
Pretty girls with their guys
Such a love you can't hide
Hey they all live for the sun

Sunsets are for lovers
And dad's and mothers
Oh and little girls
And their brothers
They all live for the sun

Go—Sun Sun Sun Sun
Sun Sun Sun Sun . . .

Parties Anyone?

Parties are just a way of life at the beach. Usually on any given Friday or Saturday night, there'd be a party somewhere at the beach or in your hometown. You usually heard of a party by word of mouth or asking around.

Sometimes you just drove around to the usual spots looking for a party. It seemed like there was always a keg of beer, sometimes they'd have a cover charge, sometimes not. If it was a BYOB, then you had to bring something or sponge off others. The music was always loud with a record/tape player or sometimes they'd have a band. Around midnight, the police would invariably come and break up the party because of the noise. Some neighbor would complain of the music or all the cars and people walking across their yard or plants. I had a pretty good sense for where the parties were. Norm claimed I could smell a party because I always managed to find one somewhere.

***Summer in Paradise*—Beach Boys**

Way back when well our master plan
Was havin' fun fun fun as America's band
Well we came out rockin' with Rhonda and Barbara Ann
Singin' of surf and sand

Now when we look back over all the fun we had
If our lifestyle's over now it sure is sad
We gotta get back to livin' without a care
Give me sunshine water and an ozone layer

Paradise is a state of mind
Where Mother Nature nurtures and man is kind
We need a change now wouldn't it be nice
If we could bring back summer

Get us back our summer
Summer in paradise(Paradise)
Summer in paradise (paradise) . . .

Beach Parties

Girls and the beach were just natural when you were a teenager. We always had a great time during our beach parties and there were always lots of girls. In the evening, we'd go to the arcade to play some games and I saw this girl with long blonde hair that was past her waist. After a few minutes, I got up the nerve to walk over and as I walked around to say something, she had a beard and mustache. I guess she was not a girl after all. That was pretty funny. The other guys thought it was a riot too. I was very leery about going over to talk to someone after that until I'd seen them from the front.

All Summer Long—*Beach Boys*

> We've been having fun
> All summer long
> All summer long
> You've been with me
> I can't see enough of you
> All summer long
> We've both been free
> Won't be long till
> Summer time is thru
>
> Every now and then
> We hear our song
> We've been having fun
> All summer long . . .

Motorcycle to the Beach

photograph by Brad Forsyth

Instrumental: Witch-tao-to-Harpers Bizarre, Brewer and Shipley

I took a girlfriend of mine, Terri, to the beach on my motorcycle one time. She hadn't been to the beach in a long time and was kind of white. I took my fins so I could do some bodysurfing. I took my friend Dan's Honda Superhawk 305. There was no backrest to it, but I couldn't take the Yamaha chopper because it was in the shop. We went to the cliffs at Balsa Chica. She lived in San Bernardino so I had about a thirty-minute drive to her house, away from the beach. Then we had a one-and-a-half-hour ride to the beach. We had a great time and got some lunch from one of the street vendors. She got a little burned and we left early enough so it wouldn't be dark by the time we got to her house. On the way home from her house, I was just driving along in the right lane of the San Bernadino Freeway when all of a sudden, a car comes flying past me, cuts in front of me, exits off the ramp, and makes a quick stop sideways. It was a good thing he did that because it was a policeman who must have noticed a car coming up the exit ramp and he blocked it from getting on the freeway going the wrong way. If he didn't, then the car would probably have gotten on just as I was going by. I wasn't able to stop so I just thanked him as I went by. I doubt that he heard me.

Little Honda—*The Hondells*

GO! I'm gonna wake you up early
Cause I'm gonna take a ride with you
We're going down to the Honda shop
I'll tell you what we're gonna do
Put on a ragged sweatshirt
I'll take you anywhere you want me to
First gear (Honda Honda) it's alright (faster faster)
Second gear (little Honda Honda) I lean right (faster faster)
Third gear (Honda Honda) hang on tight (faster faster)
Faster it's alright

It's not a big motorcycle
Just a groovy little motorbike
It's more fun that a barrel of monkeys
That two wheel bike
We'll ride on out of the town
To any place I know you like . . .

SURFING ADVENTURES
of the '60s, '70s and beyond . . .

The Graduate Movie and Horseback Riding

I used to take Carrie for rides on my motorcycle too. She was my off and on girlfriend for three years. She lived in La Verne and went to the Methodist Church there. This was the same church that was used in the move *The Graduate*. This was the scene near the end of the movie when Ben was yelling at Elaine during the end of her wedding and he is shaking the glass. She told me that the church board members were very nervous that he was going to break the glass. In fact they told the production crew if they broke the glass, they'd have to replace it. Anyway, they changed the name of the church to a Presbyterian church I believe. I took her to see the movie and when she saw her church, she yelled out "That's my church!" She was a little excited, needless to say, and embarrassed.

A couple of times, I took her for a ride on the Yamaha chopper but this one particular time, we drove around on the Honda Superhawk. There is a road north of Upland called Baseline that we used to call "the bumpy road" because there were some pretty wicked bumps along the road for a couple of miles. (It has since been leveled out.) When we were kids, our dad would take us there sometimes on a Sunday and we'd go over the bumps fairly fast and fly off our seat and sometimes bump our heads. We thought it was a blast. I took Carrie one time on the bumpy road on my motorcycle and we went over this one set of bumps and actually jumped between the two bumps. The speed limit was 35 mph but no one went that slow. To make the jump, you had to go about 70 mph. It was pretty wicked and I landed it perfectly. We went a little slower on the others but we always got a little air. Then later that day, we drove down to a place near Huntington Beach to go horseback riding along the river. I enjoyed horseback riding and used to go three to four times a week at summer camp. I think you could ride for an hour and a half for $4. It was a lot of fun. I had ridden at this place a couple of times before. Now I was used to riding my bike a lot and you'd think I'd be used to riding a horse because of all the bike riding I did but after an hour and a half of riding a horse, our butts were sore. It actually felt good to get back on the soft seat of a motorcycle.

***California Sun**—The Rivieras*

Well I'm going out West
Where I belong
Where the days are short
And the nights are long

Well they're out there having fun
In that warm California Sun . . .

To The Beach

I also took Carrie to the beach a couple of times each year. I'd go surfing while she'd read a book and caught some rays. We drove up and down the beach sometimes and at Laguna once, there was an art show in a parking lot where we stopped and checked out the paintings. One time, I brought a friend of mine, Jay, from church. This was around 1971 early in the summer and he was about to go into the Army.

***Surfer Girl**—Beach Boys*

Little surfer little one
Made my heart come all undone
Do you love me, do you surfer girl
Surfer girl my little surfer girl

I have watched you on the shore
Standing by the ocean's roar
Do you love me do you surfer girl
Surfer girl surfer girl

We could ride the surf together
While our love would grow
In my Woody I would take you everywhere I go
So I say from me to you
I will make your dreams come true
Do you love me do you surfer girl
Surfer girl my little surfer girl . . .

In the Army

About four months later, I ended up in the Army too and after going to Basic Training at Ft. Ord, I was stationed at Ft. Monmouth, NJ. I had been there about a week and was going to meet a friend of mine in a different barrack and was going through the mess hall and wouldn't you know it, there was Jay walking right towards me. We were both in shock. I found out where he was bunked and I met him and we talked about old times. A couple of weeks later, I was shipped out to Washington, DC, and I never heard from him again. Carrie and I remained good friends and wrote many times while I was in the Army. Even after my wife and I got married, we wrote and in fact, my wife and Carrie wrote many letters and became friends. We were supposed to meet her on one of our visits but were not able to get together. Unfortunately she lost her life in a car accident just a month after that. She was a great friend and I miss her warm personality and her friendship.

Instrumental: Out of Limits—The Markets

Bike Ride to the Beach

I don't know what possessed me to do this but I decided to ride my 10-speed bike to the beach one Saturday. I could have gone surfing but the waves were not really that big as I heard from listening to the radio. So I strapped on a blanket, fins, and took off for the beach. Norm worked at a grocery store near Huntington so I rode to his store and he said, "Andy, you always just seem to show up any old place, don't you?" He said he was going back to Pomona after work and that he could give me a ride back if I wanted. That was perfect because that way, I could stay at the beach a little longer. I rode the thirty miles to his work and felt pretty good. It took about two and a half to three hours to get there. I didn't take any water with me, which I should have. Then I rode the final five miles to Balsa Chica and after resting awhile I did some bodysurfing.

He was getting off at 6:00 PM so I left the beach at around 5:15 PM and made it to the store in time for him to take me back. He had a VW van so the bike could fit easily in the back.

Crutches at the Beach

A couple of weeks after I had cut my foot surfing at Balsa Chica, I was invited to stay at a beach house with a friend from church whose parents rented the house for the week. I was probably there about three or four days. I was on crutches at the time and going to the beach was tough, especially in the sand. We were at Newport so it wasn't a real long walk to the water. I remember we hung around a lot by the water and did a lot of sandcastle building or bodysurfing. I had to have my foot taped up with plastic around it because I couldn't get it wet yet. At night there would be, wall-to-wall, people on the floor but it was fun anyway. It was a bummer not being able to surf though. I had my 7' board with me. I took a chance and tried to do some bodysurfing to see if the plastic wrapping would hold up. I could walk a little but just on the side of my foot and kept the crutches near the water so I wouldn't have to go too far. On the last day, I decided to try a little surfing since the foot was healing fairly well. It was easier to surf than it was to walk. But after a few waves, the wound started to open up a little so I had to wrap it back up and wait a while before I could start surfing again.

Tow-in Skateboarding

photograph by Steve Wilkings
Hanging ten, on a skateboard! Jim Cubberley, 1965

When you can't surf or go to the beach and you weren't working, you did some other types of activities. We used to do some skateboarding because it was similar to surfing. We'd also play handball, do some weight lifting at the gym, or play on an adult basketball team. Skateboarding was the most fun. We used to do lots of tricks, but not like they do these days. Our first skateboards were homemade, out of wood, and we used old clip on roller skates to make our skateboards. We would take the skate apart and nail it onto a piece of wood. We even would put a handle on it and made a scooter out of it. But after a while, it just ended up being a skateboard again. When the first store skateboards came out, we got them and rode them until they wore out and then got another. The wheels didn't last too long but we really gave them a good workout.

Sidewalk Surfin—*Jan and Dean, The Beach Boys*

Grab your board
And you're sidewalk surfin' with me

Don't be afraid to try the trickiest sport around
Bust your buns bust your buns now
It's catchin' on in every city and town
You can do the tricks the surfers do
Kwazee moto on the sidewalk too

Grab your board
And you're sidewalk surfin' with me

You'll probably wipe out
When you first try to shoot the curve . . .

We also used to ride our bikes around, pulling each other on a skateboard. Kids today ride just about anywhere doing tricks on rails, stairs, sides of walls, half-pipes, or swimming pools with no water in them. We used to go down hills or hop in the open-type storm drains when there was no water in them. I heard of a guy who rode his surfboard down a storm drain when it was full of rushing water. I think he got arrested for that. I could see riding a kayak but not a surfboard but I guess he wanted to try it.

Warm Places

The ocean attracts people
In the summertime
And people who enjoy
Surfing in warm places
The warmth of the sun
The coolness of the wind
Relaxing from the stress
Of everyday duties

Surfing the waves
Playing in the sun
Just getting away
To warm places

Andy, 5/18/1969

11

drawing by Jane Forsyth

Hitchin' a Ride

Instrumental: Let's Go Trippin'—Dick Dale

    Hitchhiking in Southern California was a common sight in the 60s. You'd see lines of people at a freeway entrance hitchin' a ride from Southern California up to San Francisco or Berkeley University. They were usually sitting or standing near a major highway or along the coastal highway. Most of these people were so-called hippies or probably runaways. At the beach, you'd see lots of people hitchhiking. Sometimes they would have a sign as to where they were going, to get up and down the coast or up to San Francisco or other destinations. You'd even see girls hitchhiking sometimes.
    Occasionally when I didn't have a ride, I had to hitchhike as well. One weekend on a Saturday, my surfing buddies were going to Cardiff-by-the-Sea after we were done surfing at Huntington Beach but I had to work the next day. Yeah, sometimes work got in the way of surfin', and so they dropped me off on Beach Blvd at the Huntington Beach entrance with my surfboard and I had to hitchhike home. My first ride took about five

minutes to get as a guy with another board gave me a ride almost all the way up Beach Blvd. Back then, there was no 57 Orange Freeway so you had to take Imperial Avenue, then Brea Canyon to get to Diamond Bar, and then my hometown of Pomona.

It was normally about an hour-to-hour fifteen-minute drive. But it took almost three hours to get home by hitchhiking. I've made it in about two hours without a board but then sometimes, it would take four hours or more if you didn't have much luck getting a ride. One time, this lady picked me up somewhere in Orange County and asked if I'd like to meet some cool people. I was a little skeptical but I agreed anyway because she seemed nice enough. She took me to her sister's house about twenty miles farther up and not too far from the freeway where some of her relatives from out of town were there and they were getting ready to have dinner. They gave me a hamburger, hot dogs, baked beans, soft drink, and we all talked for a while. They were pretty nice but I still think it was kind of unusual that she'd ask a perfect stranger over for dinner. After that, she took me over to the freeway so I could get another ride. That was definitely a first and the only time anything like that ever happened.

I used to get picked up by a lot of people that drove a Corvette and they always seemed to like to show you how fast their car was. They'd start off fast and go even faster on the freeway.

Okay, well back to the surfboard hitchhiking story. My next ride got me to Imperial Avenue but then I was stuck for a while until a guy with a van stopped and picked me up. I did pretty good this time and got all the way to Diamond Bar. I had a few ride offers along the way but I couldn't take them because they couldn't carry a surfboard. Eventually a guy with a station wagon stopped by and I got my last ride. He was kind enough to drop me off right in front of my house. And just in time for dinner too. What timing.

There was another time; I was going to a hardware store with one of my grandmother's tenants to get something they needed to repair something in the house. He needed help carrying it so she called my mom to ask her if I could go along. He just happened to be an associate pastor for our church, Reverend Jim. Well, we were on our way home on a not-so-well-traveled road when he ran out of gas. He didn't notice how low his gas was. He wasn't used to having to hitchhike and was going to walk the three to four miles we had to go to a gas station. I suggested that we try to hitch a ride. Jim wasn't so sure but he agreed and he promptly stood there with his arm

SURFING ADVENTURES
of the '60s, '70s and beyond . . .

cocked at the elbow thumb up in the air in your classic old TV hitchhiker stance. I soon realized he had no idea how to get a ride and after a few minutes and just a few cars going by, I told him, "Why don't you let me give it a try?" He wanted to give up and just walk but I told him, "You'll have a better chance of getting a ride if you stay with the car because people will know you are having car problems and someone will be willing to help." So I gave the hitchhiking sign the way I always did by holding my arm low about waist high and thumb out, but the key is you have to look like you don't really need a ride. The second car that came by stopped and we had our ride. He took us to a gas station and along the way, we told him what happened and that Jim was a minister. He told us he was the father of two kids and took his family to church every week and he offered to wait until we got our gas and then drove us back to the car. It was very generous of him and I was sure that Jim probably was going to use this in one of his future sermons. I ran into him a few years later when he was visiting my grandmother when she was ill. The last time I saw him was at her funeral as he performed the eulogy. I reminded him of our hitchhiking adventure and he got a great chuckle out of that because he told me he used that in more than one of his sermons when the readings were about the good Samaritans or about people helping people.

Surf City—*Jan and Dean, The Beach Boys*

Two girls for every Boy

I got a 34 wagon and we call it a Woody
Surf City here we come
You know it's not very cherry
It's an oldie but a goodie
Surf City here we come
Yea it ain't got a back seat or a rear window
But it still gets me where I wanna go
They say they're never on the streets
Cause there's always something goin'
Surf City here we come
You know they're either out surfin'
Or they've got a part goin'
Surf City here we come
And if my Woody breaks down
Somewhere on the surf route
I'll strap my board to my back
And hitch a ride in my wetsuit
And when I get to Surf City
I'll be shootin' the curl
And checkin out the parties
For a surfer Girl
Surf City here we come . . .

12

drawing by Jane Forsyth

Traffic Jams, Near Misses, and Close Encounters

Encounter with a Rambler (around 1964)

We had lots of near misses and at least one close encounter. In getting to the beach, sometimes you have some problems along the way or just in the parking lot at the beach. On one of our Boy Scout trips that we took to the beach, we were in an accident on the way home. Alan and I were in the backseat facing the rear of the car of one of the parents' Station Wagon. We were on the San Diego Freeway Interstate 5 and were fast approaching stopped traffic on a Sunday afternoon. We had just stopped in the traffic jam when Alan and I saw this car coming right for us and was trying to stop. We could tell it was going to hit us. I think we yelled, "Look out we're going to get hit!" The driver looked in the mirror to see a

1962 Rambler veering to the right and plow into the back of us, probably around 20-25 mph while it was hitting the brakes. We didn't have seat belts on because there weren't any and we kind of got bounced around and our heads knocked into each other. The car had four older people in it and the ones in the backseat ended up in the front seat. Luckily no one was really hurt but they were pretty shaken up. The Rambler was another story; the front looked like an accordion. The Station Wagon only had a broken right tail light and a slightly bent rear fender. After the police came and took their accident reports, we were able to drive home. The Rambler needed a tow. We figured it probably would end up at the junk yard.

Traffic Jam Going to work

Living in Southern California, you get stuck in lots of traffic jams. It's just a part of life in the LA area. My dad would tell me that if he left home to go to work at 7:00 AM, he'd get there about 7:30 AM but if he didn't leave until 7:10 AM, he'd get there after 8:00 AM because of the volume of traffic. Coming home in the evening was no different. If you'd leave twenty to thirty minutes later, it could add one to two hours to the commute because there was always an accident somewhere. It's still that way today and a whole lot worse even though some freeways have eight lanes of traffic in BOTH directions.

Coming home from the beach one time, we were stuck in traffic earlier than usual because of an accident. I was supposed to be at work by 5:00 PM and I knew I wouldn't make it. Dave was driving the Helms bread truck so he ran me home and I got to work at 5:45 PM. I tried to explain it to my boss but he wasn't very understanding. He did let me work that night anyway.

To the Beach, Not Quite

We had a 1966 Rambler V8 that was pretty quick. I never raced it but I drove it a lot until I got my 59 Ford. Norm and I had just rented an apartment in Huntington Beach about one mile from the beach. It had a swimming pool and I was taking two of my brothers to the beach and then to my apartment to go swimming. Mike couldn't go but Chris and Brad went with me. As we were heading there on the San Bernardino Freeway near West Covina, the engine started acting strange and then stalled while I was going 65 mph and in the left lane. I lost power steering and power brakes. I had to get over to the right shoulder because there was no left shoulder. I had to avoid cars while trying to steer the car with no power or anything. I was just coasting so I put it in neutral in the hope of starting it again. I tried starting it while coasting but no luck. At first I thought I might end up running into someone but I managed to get to the right shoulder safely and stopped the car. After a few minutes, I tried to start it but didn't have any luck. It wouldn't start because the engine had frozen as we didn't have enough oil. I had just filled up the car with gas but because I didn't drive it every day and it was mainly my mom's car; I didn't check the oil. My car was in the shop, otherwise I would've taken it. My brothers stayed with the car while I walked about a half mile to the exit and got to a gas station and called my dad to tell him what happened. It was a Saturday so he wasn't working. He came to check out the car and of course he tried to start it too but it still wouldn't start. By the time the tow truck got there, it was too late to go to the beach so we never made it on that day.

Parking Lot Encounter

In San Clemente one day, we were in the parking lot and getting ready to head home after a day of surfing. We had the Helms truck all loaded and were backing out when we heard a "thump." Dave stopped and realized he'd backed into a car going by us in the parking lot. Whoops. Nothing happened to the Helms truck but the other car had a nasty dent running along the side of the car because they were going about 5 mph. Needless to say, Dave wasn't too happy. I think it may have been the same day we were stuck in traffic and I was late for work. So if we hadn't had the fender bender, I might have made it to work on time.

Bending Hoods (around spring 1966)

The craziest thing that ever happened was on one of our earlier beach trips. Dave had his dad's Blue 1955 Chevy Sedan and Dave, his brother Ed, and I were just going to go to the beach; this was just before we started surfing a lot. Well we were going to Newport to cruise around and hang out around the beach, walk, and look for some beach bunnies. We had stopped to fill up the tank and Dave checked his oil and we were on our way. The '55 Chevy was pretty cool and the ignition setup was pretty cool too because once the engine was running, you could remove the key from the ignition without the engine turning off. Well, we were driving along on the Corona Expressway when all of a sudden, the hood of the car pops right up onto the wind shield. We couldn't see anything in front of us. I quickly rolled down the window and stuck my head out so I could see and be able to tell Dave how far to move over to get to the shoulder. Fortunately, there weren't a lot of cars on the road so we made it safely to the shoulder. We were able to get the hood back down and tied it up with some rope he had in the trunk. Then we had to go back to the body shop that they take their cars to that his dad knew. We left the hood there and they told us they couldn't work on the car until next week. So we headed back to the beach. It was overcast and the waves were flat anyway so it was a good thing we didn't bring our boards. With our luck, something crazy would've happened to the boards when the hood flew up because your boards usually hang over the front of the windshield and they could've been damaged or knocked off the car. I remember one time on the freeway seeing a surfboard fly off a car and get busted up in pieces. Luckily it didn't hit another car.

Changing Lanes

On another trip, we had a close encounter when Dave was driving the '55 Chevy. Ed was in the front seat and a couple of us were in the back. We were changing lanes to the right and another car was changing into our lane too.

> I called out to Dave, "Look out another car is in the lane."
> He quickly went back into his lane and we avoided a collision.
> Dave said, "Thanks, I didn't see him moving over."
> I told him, "He started changing just before you did and you didn't realize what he was doing."

Totally Engulfed

The strangest accident I ever saw was when Norm and I were driving on the San Bernardino Freeway in LA coming back from Leo Carillo and a car was on a cement platform between a left exit onto a freeway and a right exit off the freeway. The car was laying flat on this cement platform that was at least three feet high and it was totally engulfed in flames. The owner was standing about fifty feet away on the shoulder in disbelief. It had happened moments earlier and he managed to get out and ran to the side. We stopped to make sure no one was inside and to help if we could. Not that we could at this point. That's when the guy told us it was his car. He had missed his exit and tried to exit at the last second but obviously he didn't make it. How he landed up there even he didn't know for sure. All he had was a scratch on his forehead. How lucky was that? A fire truck showed up to put out the fire and after that, we left. The police were asking if anyone saw it happen but we got there too late, we must've been there two to three minutes after it happened.

Left Turn, Stop

Now I can't let all these accidents go without telling about my motorcycle accident on the Yamaha chopper after only having it for three weeks. I was driving on a main street in town going the speed limit. I had a helmet but I wasn't wearing it and I had just bought a front fender because I didn't like dirt, mud, and pebbles getting kicked up at me all the time; it was tied onto the backseat of the bike. As I was approaching an intersection, the light had just turned green and there is a sign that reads "Watch opposing traffic on left turn." Well, the lady making a left turn didn't wait for me or the pickup truck next to me to go by before she turned. The truck was next to me, maybe about ten feet farther back in the right lane, and the lady stopped right in front me in my lane. All I could do was hit the brakes. I knew if I hit the car going 35-40 mph, I'd be hurt pretty bad or killed and I remember thinking, *it's too early; it's not my time.* When I hit the brakes, the bike went down on its right side and somehow, my right leg got out and over on the left side of the bike. So here I was sitting on the left side of the bike as the back of my bike passed under the front of her car without hitting it and my body just missing the car by inches. The bike finally stopped after about fifty feet but I kept going another thirty feet or so bouncing on my butt. I popped up and ran back to my bike to turn it off but I couldn't get to the key because the front of the truck was on top of my bike. If I didn't get off the bike, I'd have been pinned under the truck. The truck backed off and I turned off the bike and then yelled at the lady because I was understandably a little angry. My anger didn't last too long because I realized how lucky I was to have survived what just happened and without being seriously injured.

Her insurance covered the repairs to my bike and also gave me some money to cover possible expenses for my injuries. I didn't want much, just enough in case I had some problems, but all I ended up with was a sore butt and scratched ankle. I got the bike back in three weeks and was back riding again. I was surfing the next weekend after the accident.

Loose Surfboards on the Freeway

I mentioned earlier about seeing a surfboard go flying off a car on the freeway but fortunately not hitting any other cars.

Going to San Clemente one day on the San Diego Freeway, I only had the Royal Hawaiian surfboard with me and I guess I didn't have the wooden rack too secure. As I was driving along the freeway with the windows open, I always checked periodically to see if the board was okay. I reached up and didn't feel the board. I was about fifteen minutes from San Clemente. I immediately had this flash of seeing my board flying up in the air and busting apart as it hit the freeway and seeing other cars plowing into it. I looked over my shoulder to the right and could see the tail of the board bouncing around so I immediately, but carefully, pulled over on the right shoulder and none too soon. The back rack was barely hanging on. I refastened it and was good the rest of the way. That was too close.

Leaking Valve Stem

In the fall of 1970, I went to Corona del Mar after my last class of the day which ended at 12:30 PM. I studied for a couple of hours sitting there enjoying the nice weather, then got my board and did some surfing on the small- to medium-sized waves for a couple of hours while the sun was still up.

I was getting my board loaded on my car and noticed that my right rear tire was a little low. So I went to a gas station and put some air in the tire, but I noticed that the valve stem had a slow leak. I drove for about twenty minutes and then stopped again to check the tire and it was low again. I only had $1.75 and when I asked the service station attendant if they could replace the valve stem, they said it would cost $3.00. I told them I only had $1.75 and would come back with the money later, that

I only lived about forty minutes away. But they wouldn't do it. I figured I should be able to make it home by stopping at a gas station about every twenty minutes.

When I got on the Corona Expressway, there was some road work going on and as I was passing it, the tire blew out. I started to swerve and I hit the brakes and as I was slowing down, I thought for a moment that I might go down into the construction ditch which was about a six-foot hole and about 40 to 50 feet long on the right shoulder. I was lucky that I was able to keep it under control until I pulled over. I would have changed the tire but I didn't have a spare tire.

I had another car, a 51 Ford that I bought for $50 that had the same size tires and it had a spare tire. I locked up the car and figured I'd have to hitchhike home. It took about ten minutes before someone stopped and wouldn't you know, it was a truck carrying a bunch of chickens. I couldn't sit in the cab of the truck because the guy had his two big dogs up there with him. So there I was riding in the back of a truck with a bunch of chickens, sitting in chicken shit, and it smelled really bad back there too. He dropped me off at the south end of town and I eventually got a lift to the main road in town and I walked the rest of the way.

I called Dan and we drove my 51 Ford to my car and I got the tire changed. The next day, I bought two new tires and used my left rear tire as a spare tire. Lesson learned, have a good spare tire and carry enough cash in case of emergencies.

13

drawing by Jane Forsyth

Staying in Surfing Shape

Skateboarding and other Sports

In order to keep your surfing skills sharp when you weren't surfing, you'd do other activities like skateboarding, swimming, weight lifting, running, or just playing other sports like baseball, handball, basketball, volleyball, football, ping-pong, foosball, even shooting some pool. Anything competitive was good for keeping you sharp. In thinking back, I don't think we consciously did these things to stay sharp for surfing; we did all these things to keep from not doing anything. We always were doing something when we weren't working, partying, surfing, or occasionally studying.

At the college I went to, we had lots of hills and I noticed some guys would ride their skateboard to class. This was great because you could get there faster. Sometimes, the way your schedule might be arranged you may not have enough time to make it because the classes were so far apart. So I'd say there were about three or four of us who'd ride our skateboards to class. Sometimes you'd have to dodge and cut around people so you wouldn't run into them. It was even easier going uphill because of the momentum you got by kicking your foot while on the board. Except for this one hill that was really steep. You really didn't want to go down that hill with people around. But I did want to try it out sometime to see how fast I could go. So on a Saturday when I had to do some research at the library, I had my board with me and gave the hill a try. Now the skateboards back then weren't quite as good as they are now but I got up some pretty good speed until the board started to shake and I hung in for as long as I could until I had to bail out. I ran to a stop, but the board kept going and eventually stopped when it traveled onto the grass at the bottom of the hill. I actually made it down three fourths of the hill which was about 200 yards long, I estimated. I probably got up to 25 mph maybe only 20, but it could have been faster than 25—it's hard to tell.

I also used to skateboard a lot around the front of our house doing tricks, jumps, hard left and right cuts much like they do today; but the kids today are many levels above what we did back then. Even the best skateboard riders who entered competitions weren't nearly as talented as the kids of today and the tricks that they can do. Probably because the equipment is so much better now. But we had fun and it also helped us to keep up our surfing skills.

Lifesaving

One summer I took a lifesaving course in the hopes of getting a job as a lifeguard at the local pool or even the beach. It was a very tough course and of the twenty-five kids in the class only two of us were able to pass the course. Then later that summer I joined a swim team to help with my swimming conditioning. It was hard to stay with it because we practiced five times a week and the meets were on Saturday. So after three weeks and one swim meet I had to drop out because not only did I have to work but I wanted to get in my surfing and work. I kept up my swimming at the local pool getting in 40 to 50 laps a day when I could. Some of the serious big wave surfers of today even practice staying underwater for long periods of time by running underwater carrying heavy objects like 50 lb rocks or weights.

Weight Lifting

Another activity we did was weight lifting. We would go at least three times a week to the gym, usually late in the evening after work. Sometimes we'd do leg workouts with weights on the off day and get in some running as well, usually about two to three miles. The owners got to know us pretty well and we became friends with them. After the first year, he said he wouldn't charge us if while we were doing our workouts we helped the other guys. Kind of what the personal trainers do today. As long as we came there at least three times a week. We were almost always there three to five times a week anyway so that wasn't a problem. One day I was trying my max on the bench at 280 lbs. I only weighed 155 at the time. I couldn't quite get it up but I said I'll make it next time in about five minutes. Well the owner was the one spotting me and he knew that if you missed a heavy attempt, then you probably couldn't make it next time because your muscles were burned out. So he told me if I made it, he'd give me $5. It wasn't a bet because I wasn't betting anything. Maybe it was the incentive I needed because when I tried my next attempt, I made it although it wasn't easy.

A Gallon of Milk

Another time at the gym, the guys were talking about the fact that you couldn't drink a gallon of milk in an hour. One guy said he tried it and missed by about two cups. Well, guess who thought they could do it? Yes, yours truly. But the attempt wasn't going to be for two days because I had just eaten. So I did a lot of eating to try and expand my stomach and drank lots of milk. I usually drank a lot of milk anyway, sometimes a quart at one time so I honestly thought I could do it. This also wasn't a bet but the two guys that thought I couldn't do it would buy the milk and give me $10 each if I succeeded. If not, then I had to buy the milk. When the day arrived, they showed up with half and half milk and I told them no way it had to be whole milk in quart containers so they went back and got them. Then I started. I hadn't eaten for eight hours so I was definitely empty. I got down the first two quarts in about twenty minutes. I didn't want to rush. The problem with milk is that it has to digest like food and that it takes a little more than an hour to digest. The third quart took about twenty minutes and I was feeling full. I tried a little stationary

SURFING ADVENTURES
of the '60s, '70s and beyond . . .

bike to try and make some room but I think that just churned it up more. Then they started trying to make me sick by saying things like green cheese tastes so good, sour milk will make you puke, buttermilk is sour and tastes like vomit, cottage cheese is really rotten milk, anything to try and make me queasy. Then with about fifteen minutes left, I started the last quart and got about two thirds of it down with five minutes left but the other condition was that I had to keep it down. Well as stubborn as I was, I didn't give up. I went to the backdoor where there was a storm drain because I knew it was coming up. I got the last of it down with less than a minute to go but then it just wouldn't stay down and I lost it all. I'll tell you one thing, I felt a whole lot better after I lost it but I'll never try that again. Now even though I didn't win, they couldn't believe I actually got it all down. We had some great laughs about it and I couldn't drink milk for a long time after that.

Basketball, Baseball, and Ping-Pong

Some of us also played team sports too like basketball or baseball. I played on the local Pony and Colt baseball teams and also on the Church basketball team and later on an adult basketball team. When I was in junior high and high school, we used to go to our high school gym during the summer to play some ping-pong or some pickup basketball games. I used to play ping-pong a lot when I was younger because we had a table at home. It was fun to play against other people who were pretty good and really helped your reflexes and hand to eye coordination.

Handball and Racquetball

Our college also had six handball courts where we could play handball. For two semesters, I signed up for the handball class and got pretty good. We were playing one time in the evening and saw these two guys on the last court playing a game using what looked like sawed of tennis racquets and the bigger red handball. Beginner handball players used these big red balls because they were softer and easier on the hands. Then you would switch to the smaller harder black ball when you were better and your hands were used to the pounding. We watched these paddle racquet players for a few minutes and we decided it wasn't much fun or much of a workout and you could only use one hand and you could get hurt if someone hit you with the racquet. It wasn't like tennis where you are across the net. The two of them were in the same court together right next to each other. Well this game they were playing, we figured, wouldn't catch on because it didn't look as challenging as handball.

Our football coach used to play one wall paddleball with the other coaches after practice using a tennis ball. Well that "sport" called paddle racquet evolved into racquetball. And in 1975, while attending college at the University of MD, I signed up for a handball/racquetball class and got my first taste of racquetball. I won the class-ending handball tournament and was in the semifinals of the racquetball tournament and the instructor was watching us and noticed I was changing hands with the racquet in the middle of the rally. After all, there wasn't a string (or tether) on the racquets back then. He told me I couldn't change hands in the middle of the rally. I finished the game with one hand and won but lost in the finals because I didn't have much of a backhand. I didn't play RB again until 1979. I started playing nearly every day and have enjoyed playing racquetball for over thirty years now.

In 2006, I participated in National Championships playing in the 50+ OPEN division and the 45+A Division. I made the finals of the 45+A consolation round and I lost to Rueben Gonzalez in the round of sixteen. He won the 45+ and 50+ divisions and is a former number one professional racquetball player. Racquetball is a great sport that you can play for a long time all year around as long as you're healthy enough.

Pictures, Paintings and Drawings

Photographs by Steve Wilkings
www.stevewilkings.com

Dana Point, 1964, unknown surfer

Carlsbad, 1965, Tandem Surfing

Secos, 1965, Jim Cubberley

Wheelie on Skateboard, 1965, Jim Cubberley

Huntington Beach, 1965, Gary Propper

Huntington Beach, 1966, David Nuuhiwa

Hermosa, 1966, "Hanging Heels"

Hermosa Beach, 14th Street, 1966, Sparky Hudson & Crazy Kate

SURFING ADVENTURES
of the '60s, '70s and beyond...

Carlsbad Surf Contest, 1966,
Bay Cities Surf Club
surfers and spectators

San Clemente, 1966, Sparky Hudson

San Clemente, 1966, David Nuuhiwa

Mexico, K-38, 1966, Ken Rocky

Waxing a board, 1966, Juicy James Café

Three surfers walking along the beach

Malibu, 1967, Fletcher Sharp

Malibu, 1967, Tom Padaca

SURFING ADVENTURES
of the '60s, '70s and beyond...

Santa Barbara Campus Point, 1968, Mike Purpus

Hermosa Beach, 1969, Steve Clark

Hermosa Beach, 1970, Keith Paull & Russel Hughes

Hermosa Beach, 1970, Mike Purpus

Photographs by Jane Forsyth

Playing in the sand, mid 50s Andy & Chris, Newport Beach, late 50s

Chris, Andy, Brad, Mike in football pileup, Huntington Beach, early 60s

Cooking HotDogs at a Huntington Beach fire ring, sometime around 1978.

SURFING ADVENTURES
of the '60s, '70s and beyond...

Lifeguard stand at Leo Carillo State Park, early 60s

Checking out the waves, this is where Burt Lancaster & Debra Kerr filmed a scene "From Here to Eternity", Leo Carillo, early 60s

Where we saw Buddy Ebsen at Leo Carillo, early 60s

Leo Carillo all four of us down there, Leo Carillo, early 60s

Mike with Chris's 8'6" Hobbie, Leo Carillo, 1970

Andy ready to hit the waves, Leo Carillo, 1970

Andy with the Royal Hawaiian surfboard. 1969

unknown photographer
Andy & Lee relaxing at Newport Beach on a church beach trip, checking out the scenery with binoculars

SURFING ADVENTURES
of the '60s, '70s and beyond . . .

Catchin' a wave at Leo Carillo (Andy on the left), 1969

Catchin a wave, Andy, Leo Carillo, 1969

End of a ride, Andy, Leo Carillo, 1970

artist Jane Forsyth
Painting that my mom did in 1972 of the surfing area at Leo Carillo entitled "Surfers Paradise"

photograph by Brad Forsyth
Andy's 1967 Yamaha Motorcycle used to carry the 7' surfboard to the beach

photograph by Norm Broyle
Andy's 1967 Yamaha with the Hat & Jacket bought during the Mexico trip while in Tijuana, 1971

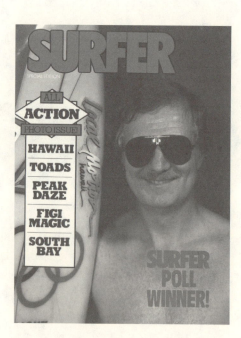

A mock picture of Andy on the cover of a surfing magazine, MGM DisneyWorld, 1988

SURFING ADVENTURES
of the '60s, '70s and beyond . . .

internet open source

A 60s Chevy Panel Truck, similar to the Helms Bread Truck we had only ours was a cream yellow color

photographer Andy Forsyth
an old VW bug like Charlie's

internet open source
old surfboards in a truck

Paintings by Bruno Turpin
www.surfarts.com

These paintings are featured at the beginning of many of the chapters throughout the book.

AlbiNose

Waimea Drop

Surfer Ricon, un reve . . .

SURFING ADVENTURES
of the '60s, '70s and beyond...

Franck session

Bottum turn

Nose Beaute

The Style

Nose Riding

Glassy Morning

SURFING ADVENTURES
of the '60s, '70s and beyond . . .

Photographs by Andy Forsyth

2008 Seal Beach
Some long boarders

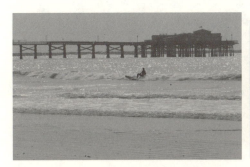

This guy had been surfing since 1960

2008 The cliffs at Balsa Chica

The guy from San Francisco and his dog

SURFING ADVENTURES
of the '60s, '70s and beyond...

2008 Huntington Beach

Beach Volleyball

Huntington Pier, can you imagine the waves going over the end of the pier

Huntington Beach Factory, the smoke is much cleaner now than it used to be

The Wedge

The Wedge on a small day

Crystal Cove, the scene of
Senior ditch day

Laguna Beach

SURFING ADVENTURES
of the '60s, '70s and beyond...

Andy's surfing buddies and friends,

all pictures are from our 1969 PHS yearbook, unless otherwise noted.

Track Team Andy & Dave
Andy 2nd row from top, 4th from left
Dave, next to Andy, 3rd from left

Motorcycle Club, my cousin is Sam, second from left
I actually bought this bike in the summer of 1969, an 80cc Yamaha dirt bike. The guy I bought it from is on the left.

Golf Club

Surf and Ski Club at Pomona High School, 1969
Most of us were members but none of us are in the picture.

Andy

photograph by Jane Forsyth
Taken just a couple weeks before going into the Army at a family reunion in Riverside, Calif, 120 degrees that day.

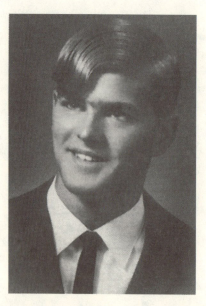

Dave

courtesy of Dave
Dave recent picture on his sailboat

SURFING ADVENTURES
of the '60s, '70s and beyond . . .

Ed, Dave's younger brother

Charlie (not the Charlie with the VW)

Gary

Leo

Sefo (the Hawaiian)

Chris (not my brother)

Pete

My good friend from Boy Scouts and High School. Used my surfboard as a belly board.

SURFING ADVENTURES
of the '60s, '70s and beyond . . .

Photographs of Hawaii

Kauai Surf Resort, from our Hotel, 1973

photographs by Andy Forsyth

photograph by Cecelia Forsyth
Andy with rental board, Waikiki, 1973

photograph by Marilyn Estep
Andy and new long board taken at Cheeseburger in Paradise, Pasadena, MD, (2008)

photograph by Cecelia Forsyth
Waikiki, I'm out there somewhere

photograph by Andy Forsyth
Diamond Head, looking across Waikiki Beach

2008 Pictures of the same resort in Kauai
Photographs by Brad and Colleen Forsyth
Jan. 2008

Kauai Surf Resort, same place we stayed in 1973

surfing in the bay   surfing in the bay

Andy Forsyth

Paintings by Garry Birdsall
www.surfart.com.au

Sunrise Surf   First Surf of the Day

Surf Session

SURFING ADVENTURES
of the '60s, '70s and beyond...

Worth the Drive

Reef Break

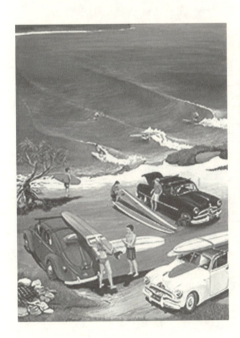

Ground Swell

55 Chevy Bel-Air

Beach Break

Urban Surf

Rover 4x4

Beetle

SURFING ADVENTURES
of the '60s, '70s and beyond...

Off the Beaten Track

Reef Café

Bus to Nowhere

Holden Ute'

Surf Bug

Woodie

SURFING ADVENTURES
of the '60s, '70s and beyond . . .

Last Surf of the Day

Sunset Surf

2007 Mavericks

Photographs by Andy Forsyth

Mavericks Truck out front of the Surf Shop

Mural in the Maverick Surf Shop

old Mavericks surf boards, most were Jeff Clark's

14

drawing by Jane Forsyth

Oh, That's Gotta Hurt

Every surfer, if they have surfed for a while, eventually gets injured or nearly drowns. Some sustain serious injuries, say after an attempt to shoot the pier or while surfing between a couple of rocks. Or while surfing big waves like at the Pipeline in Hawaii and end up slamming into the coral reefs on the bottom and getting cut up, suffer a broken collar bone, broken arm, fractured ribs, or a concussion.

Really big waves are dangerous just because of the pure power of the waves and the massive amount of water that is being thrust over the top and the distance to the bottom that you are being driven downward. It's sort of like going over a large waterfall but even worse. These waves can keep you down so long that it is difficult to get to the surface. And when you do surface, the next wave could be ready to drop on you and you don't have any time to get a breath. People have drowned surfing really big waves, even smaller ones, people have suffered some pretty serious injuries too including paralysis.

There is a guy, Jesse Billauer in Encinitas, California, who suffered a spinal cord injury while surfing and is confined to a wheelchair because he can't walk. He was a world-class amateur competitive surfer. He's surfing again but on a specially made board that he rides laying on his stomach and on smaller waves with the help of his friends. Now that is true friendship. It's great that he doesn't let his disability keep him from doing what he enjoys doing.

In surfing, injuries happen but sometimes an injury occurs that could have been prevented. I was at Balsa Chica, which is just north of Huntington State and City Beaches, with my brother, Chris, and a friend of his, Sean. I was out surfing some moderate-sized waves and enjoying the day and getting some nice rides. But on this one wave I was riding in, there were a couple of cute girls in the water so I zigzagged around them and was going to go back to talk to them. I jumped off my board and landed right on a broken bottle. "Oh, shit, that hurts," I yelled to myself. I knew immediately what had happened because I had stepped on a broken bottle before in the sand and gotten a little cut but nothing like this. I usually never jump off my surfboard; I usually do a kickout and turn around. Why I jumped off? I'll never know.

I made it to the shore and looked down at the bottom of my left foot to see a four-inch long deep cut on the bottom of it. Well my day of surfing was over, but I didn't want to go home right away because it was still early in the day and my brother was here with his friend. I was able to make it up to where the food trailers were and they had some first aid tape so I patched it up as best I could and we hung around for about two more hours. By around 1:30 PM, it was hurting too much so I told my brother I needed to get home to our doctor and get it stitched up. Fortunately, it was my left foot so I could still drive.

We packed up everything, loaded up the surfboard, and headed home. What a bummer. My foot was killing me by now and we wouldn't be able to enjoy the rest of this beautiful summer day.

I made it back in record time and dropped off my brother's friend. Then we went to the doctor. I was able to get right in to see him. Of course he asked how it happened and I told him that I thought I stepped on a broken bottle in the ocean. He agreed that's what it probably was. This could have been avoided by the person just throwing away the bottle in a trash can. I hoped no one else stepped on it but there were so many people around I don't think they could have avoided it. Needless to say, I avoided that area in the future.

The doctor gave me a local Novocain and when it was numb, he came back and was preparing to stitch me up.

He said, "Okay, turn your head now because I'm going to start stitching."

I told him, "No way, I'm going to watch to make sure you do it right."

He just laughed and said, "Okay."

Since it was totally numb, I didn't feel it anyway and after eight stitches, he was done. He gave me a set of crutches and my brother and I went home.

I couldn't work for about three weeks because I worked at a grocery store and couldn't stand. I belonged to the union so I got workman's compensation for the time I was off. After about three weeks, I tried surfing even though it wasn't completely healed. I could actually surf better than I could walk because it hurt to take a step. It opened up a little so I laid off surfing for another week. By the fourth week, it was healed enough that I could get around better and go back to work and resume my surfing. I was able to start running again after a couple of more weeks.

If people would just throw away their trash in the trash cans, then things like this wouldn't happen; but I guess when you're drunk, it seems like fun to just toss your bottles in the ocean. Maybe they'll step on one someday and know what's it's like. We can only hope.

Surfin Bird—The Trashmen

Well everybody's heard about the Bird
Bird bird bird b-bird is the word
Well bird bird bird birds is a word
Well bird bird bird birds is a word
Well bird bird bird birds is a word

Don't you know about the bird
Well a bird bird bird bird is the word
Everybody knows that the bird is a word

Surfer bird whowoslowkwowkwk aaaaahhhh
Papa Papa Papa Papa ooom mow mow
Papa ooom mow mow
Papa ooom mow mow
Papa ooom mow mow

Well Don't you know about the bird
Everybody knows that the bird is a word
Papa ooom mow mow
Papa ooom mow mow
Papa ooom mow mow
Papa ooom mow mow

Surfer bird whowoslowkwowkwk aaaaahhhh . . .

15

drawing by Andy Forsyth

When You Gotta Go

You're out there on the water and the waves are really kicking. You're out maybe a half mile or more and it took you maybe twenty minutes to get out and make it through the breakwater. When you have the urge to go. Nobody talks about it but everyone has done it. You know that if you paddle in to take care of business, it'll be another half hour or longer before you can get back out so you say screw it I'll just go here and then you catch the next wave.

But what happens when it's not that simple and you have to really go, both ways. Nobody talks about that either. Well there's lots of fish out there and they don't run ashore to do their business; what about a whale, what do they do? So we'd just paddle out away from the lineup, hang on the board, and let it out. Now it isn't something that happens every day, but when you gotta go, you gotta go, just go away from everyone else.

(An article in one of the Surfer Magazines appeared that talked about this and I actually wrote these paragraphs a few months before I read the article).

Sailing We Will Go

I want to take you on a trip
Across oceans near and far
I want to take you sailing
To surf in the sun and under the stars

We'll take a journey on our sailing boat
To lands we've never seen
We'll meet people playing music
And surfin' places we've never been

The places that we'll go
And the places that we'll surf
Will stay etched upon our minds
And forever they will be

Sailing, Surfing, Sailing we will go
We'll take a trip across the sea
There's no other place I'd rather go
So come sail and surf with me

There's no place I'd rather be
Than sailing with you
There's nowhere I'd care to be
So come along and surf with me

Andy, 2/20/2007

16

drawing by Jane Forsyth

Red Water and Smokey Skies

    The eeriest thing I ever experienced when surfing or any other time for that matter was around the summer of 1970, when there were over ten thousand brush and forest fires throughout Southern California. Every year, there are brush fires but this year, because of the dry conditions and high winds, the fires spread quickly and were nearly impossible to contain. (This also happened again this past summer of 2007.) There were so many fires that a cloud of smoke just hung over the entire valley. Even though it was early summer and the middle of the day, you had to drive with your lights on because it was that dark. A kind of dark reddish brown haze came through as the sun tried to make its way through all the smoke. I decided to try and get away from the smoke for the day and headed down to the beach to go surfing, hoping that the offshore breezes would keep the smoke away from the ocean. Ash was falling from the skies and if you let your car sit for an hour, it was covered with ash. Driving to the beach was very strange with ash flying around almost like a light snowfall. It kind of smelled like a dirty fireplace and I couldn't wait to get to the beach where I hoped it would be better.

South Bay Surfer—Beach Boys

Look out here come those South Bay surfers
California's gettin' hot
There they go cruisin' down that coastline
Lookin' for their favorite spot

We'll find the big one

Oh the boys are rough and
Ready to handle anything
They take the big one
You'll catch 'em surfing . . .

After finally arriving at the beach, it wasn't too bad, but you could see the smoke approaching. After about an hour in the water, the smoke finally crept overhead and with the sun shining through the clouds, the water looked red. It almost seemed like you were sitting in a big ocean of blood, very eerie. Then pretty soon the ashes started falling. If you sat waiting too long for a wave, your board would start getting covered in ash and so would you. I got a few waves but eventually gave up. I drove further south but couldn't get away from the smoke and ash. So I just went back home since I had to work later in the afternoon anyway. I needed to take a shower to get all the ashes off but it didn't matter much because it got right back on you when you went outside. The next morning, the cars were covered in about a half inch to an inch of ash. I had never seen anything like this. In a couple of days, things were getting back to normal as the fires were getting under control and the rains came and the Santa Anna winds subsided. Definitely something I'll never forget; it was a very eerie experience.

17

painting by Bruno Turpin

Surfin' in the Snow

    We used to sleep on the beach north of Huntington Beach at a place called Balsa Chica. You would park along the road or the small parking lot or up on the cliff and make your way down the steps to the beach. You could sleep on the beach because there was no curfew or lifeguards. There were some fire rings so you could have a fire going if you brought some firewood. The fire rings were old and not nearly as good as the ones at Huntington State Beach.

Melekalikimaka—Beach Boys

It's been my secret passion to try it
To spend my Christmas surfin', I can't deny it
I wanna spend my Christmas on the Kona Coast in Hawaii

For years I saved my pennies and planned it
The great Pacific Ocean, we'll span it
I wanna spend Christmas where I dig it the most, in Hawaii

Winter in the sun and surf'd sure be nice
In a south sea garden paradise
I wanna spend Christmas where I dig it the most, in Hawaii

Honolulu, Waikiki
Do you wanna come along with me?
Waimea up to Hanalai
I'd love to take you to the islands today . . .

We'd just find a spot near a fire ring but far enough away from the water so you wouldn't get hit by high tide. Maybe build up the sand to protect yourself from the wind, climb in your sleeping bed, and crash. Then again sometimes we'd just party half the night. On New Year's Eve one year, we got a bunch of us together for a party and we stayed up pretty late playing songs on our guitars, listening to music on the radio, or just getting a little bombed. In the morning we'd struggle to get up and get ready to go surfing. No breakfast unless the guys with the food carts were there. We just headed out to the water to surf. Some of us had wet suits, because it was January and it was a little cold. But it did wake you up when you hit the water. After about twenty minutes, your fingers were kind of purple and after an hour, you were pretty numb. You'd have to get out of the water and get warmed up by a fire. Then out you'd go again. After two to three hours, everyone was pretty much drained because it took a lot out of you surfing in cold water.

Then someone had an idea. I don't remember who it was but someone said, "Let's go up to the Mountains and go skiing."

So we all agreed and we packed up all our gear and surfboards and decided to go to Big Bear because it was the closest. Less than two hours

SURFING ADVENTURES
of the '60s, '70s and beyond...

later, we were at the mountain. A week ago, they just had a good snowfall and the roads were open again.

Where else can you go surfing in the morning, drive a couple of hours and go skiing in the afternoon? Not all of us could ski so some of us decided, before we got there, to take the fins off our boards and go down the toboggan runs on our surfboards. Great idea, so while we were driving up, we were figuring out what we were going to do and how to go down the trails on our boards. After we got there, a few guys took off for the trails to ski and the rest of us found the toboggan trails. We waited for the toboggan and sled riders to clear and we took off on a surfboard; four of us on one board just like a toboggan. We didn't have brakes so we had to put out our feet to try and stop. We didn't stop very well and kind of tumbled off with bodies flying everywhere and the board flipping over almost hitting one of us in the head. It was a blast. So we headed up again and this time we decided to go down one at a time, standing up, like we were surfing. There was just one minor problem that we hadn't thought of or figured out yet and that was how to stop. The first guy took off and it wasn't long before he was going pretty fast and we all realized at the same time, how's he going to STOP! So we all watched as he got near the end of the run he must have thought of it too as he shouted "How do I stop!" And we all yelled back "Jump!" and he bailed out rolling down the hill like a wipe out in the water except that he came up all covered in white snow. He finally stopped but the board kept going until it hit a bush, flipped up and over. He picked himself up, retrieved his board, and he looked liked a big snowball covered in snow. It was great and we were all juiced and ready to take our turn. Then the next guy took off. This time he had an idea and sat down on the board near the end and tried to stop by digging in his feet. It kind of worked but he slid off the board and rolled to a stop anyway. But the board didn't. We all took a few turns on the trails in between the tobogganers, who, by the way, were having a big thrill watching us ride our boards down the hill and going into hysterics every time we tried to stop and essentially ended in a massive wipe out.

After about an hour or so, a ranger came by and saw what we were doing and told us to stop because we could hurt someone or ourselves riding those boards down the hill. So I guess our fun was over. But we hiked around until we found a place where there weren't any tobogganers or sleders and started going down the hill there. We had a great time but when it got dark, we had to stop. So we packed away the boards and headed to the lodge to wait for the rest of the guys. It was probably a good thing the ranger stopped us because we could have gotten seriously hurt if we hit a tree or rock or someone else. The other spot, we found, was a little safer and there was no one else around. I'd like to think that one of the people that saw us that day created a real snowboard and that was the start of snowboarding, but who knows. It was around 1970 and I'm not sure when snowboarding started. The biggest problem was stopping and turning because we didn't have an edge to turn and we weren't strapped in so we couldn't steer the thing in the direction we wanted to go. We just went straight down the hill fast. It was a blast, but it was also the only time we ever went snow surfing.

An Amazing World

Mountains are one of the most
Amazing parts of our world
They can soar as high as
Nearly 6 miles above sea level
And can be freezing cold with snow
Even in the summer

The ocean is one of the most
Amazing parts of our world
It can spread as wide as
5000 miles across
And bring us some amazing waves
Big, small or perfectly formed

Wind is one of the most
Amazing parts of our world
It can travel for
Thousands of miles across the sea
Just to bring us waves to surf

SURFING ADVENTURES
of the '60s, '70s and beyond . . .

Snow is one of the most
Amazing parts of our world
It can pile up to
20 or 30 feet high
In just a few days
And is very beautiful

You can ski in the deep powder
Snowboard down the slopes
Toboggan or go tubing
Or do what we did
Take the fins off your surfboard
And surf the snow

Surfing is one of the most
Amazing things you can do
Even the mountains cannot keep away the surfers
No ocean is wide enough
The wind cannot stop from forming the waves
The snow cannot cover the ocean

Nothing in this world can keep
Surfers from the waves

Andy, 12/18/2006

18

painting by Bruno Turpin

Safe Water or Not and Bad Air

Looking back at some of the places we would surf, I'd have to question how safe some of them were. I remember as a kid, we would come back from the water after playing in the surf and the waves and we'd have this black stuff on the bottom of our feet. We'd ask our dad what that was and he said it was tar that came off the ships. They still have that problem today but I don't think it's quite as bad. The water also wasn't what I'd call the cleanest looking because it was a kind of brownish green and there was a lot of foam, almost like it was soapy water. I think that was due to the alkaline level in the water combined with the warm temperature and salt water.

But the most peculiar and potentially harmful location for your health was near Golden West right next to Balsa Chica. I remember surfing along the cliffs and the water was a little cold and then I saw some good break maybe 50 to 100 yards over and so I paddled over and the water was nice and warm. I stayed there for a couple of hours and the waves were pretty good. Occasionally I'd drift over a little and the water felt cold again so I'd go back to where it was warm. It took a while before I thought to look and see where the warm water was coming from and I noticed these large drainage openings maybe six or eight feet coming from the cliffs and realized it was the water runoff that was used to cool the oil refineries across the highway or possibly the storm drains from the city. So at first I thought; *this can't be good but then if the water was really bad, wouldn't there be signs warning us of hazardous waters conditions?* So I continued to surf there and I guess since I didn't get cancer, no limbs have fallen of or anything, 40 years later, it must have been okay.

I know there were some places where you weren't allowed to go on the beach because of bad water. But then, wouldn't the whole area be contaminated? How would they be able to confine it to just that one beach? At least they didn't have the problems they do now with oil spills and garbage and hypodermic needles and other stuff. Then they put up a nuclear power plant on the coast near Santa Onofre in the 70s and I'm sure that affected the environment and the water as well.

I don't know exactly what they were manufacturing in Huntington Beach at the factories but there were and still are lots of oil derricks around but not all are active anymore. My guess is that it was some kind of oil refinery and they were always working and pouring out grey and sometimes black smoke into the air. I was out there recently and it looked like they must have installed some pollution control devices because the smoke was minimal and white rather than black. That was another big problem in the late 50s, 60s, and into the 70s—the air pollution.

I remember playing in our backyard as a kid about 9 years old and a feeling in my chest like someone stabbing me with a knife when it was just the dense smog. Most of the days, you couldn't see the mountains just fifteen to twenty miles away from our house in Pomona. On a clear day, you could see the mountains from the ocean, probably 50 to 60 miles away. I remember one day, I looked out and couldn't see the houses across the street and it wasn't fog—it was the SMOG. Sometimes it would get so bad I'd just get in my car or motorcycle and go to the beach. It always seemed to be better down there because of the winds. After a few bad days of smog, the winds would blow the smog out over the ocean and you could see offshore all the brown stuff just hovering out there and then eventually dissipate.

California has done a pretty good job over the last thirty years of cleaning up the air by implementing the strictest pollution control devices on the cars, buses, trucks, and factories and are working towards encouraging alternate energy sources.

I believe my surfing has given me a better sense of environment awareness and a desire to see cleaner air and water and shorelines. After all, who wants to surf in garbage, hazardous water, waste, and dangerous materials floating in the water and emitting potentially harmful chemicals into the water and air and injuring or killing our marine animals and land-based animals?

19

photograph by Norm Broyle

Motorcycles and Surfboards

    I guess we all go through certain phases in our lives when we have to do something or have something and that driving force is so strong that sometimes it clouds our better judgment. Besides surfing, which for me was a passion and a fun thing to do, I became interested in wanting to own a motorcycle. I'm not really sure why other than the sense of freedom you get with no doors or roof, the wind blowing in your face and all around you. So I set out to get a motorcycle. I didn't really know much about them or what kind I wanted so I didn't really know where to look. When I told my parents that I wanted to get one, they were opposed to it and didn't think it was a good idea. But being 18 now, I knew more than my parents and didn't really have to listen to them; a lot like most kids back then and now too for that matter. So I heard about a guy in my school who was selling a Yamaha 80cc dirt bike for $150 so I gave him a call. He was in the motorcycle club at school and was pretty good on the bike. He used to ride it in dirt contests. Now I had never ridden a bike before so he had to teach me. I got pretty good at it and so I bought the bike and started riding a lot. I used it to get to and from work and to other places and rode in the dirt some too. It was a street legal bike but didn't have any lights. My friend Dan and I tried to hook up the lights but we didn't have a clue as to what we were doing so after about an hour we gave up.

    A couple months later, Dan bought a Honda 305 Superhawk, which I took care of when he went in the service about a year later. I kept the dirt bike for about six months and then sold it for $125. But I still had the desire to ride a motorcycle. Then one day, I saw this guy go buy on a chopper. It had a set of drawback handle bars, an orange and yellow flame teardrop gas tank, a long backrest, and a big rear tire. I didn't know what kind of bike it was but it was just what I was looking for. I found out later, when I was at work talking about the bike, that one of the cashiers said it sounded like the kind of bike her brother had and that he was selling it. He was also the older brother of Sean, my Brother Chris's friend who I took to the beach when I cut my foot. So I gave the guy a call and went to see the bike and gave it a test ride. It was a Yamaha 320 cc scrambler dirt bike that had been modified into a street chopper. Plus it was a lot less expensive than the cost of a stock Harley Davidson, let alone a modified Harley chopper. My mom wasn't too crazy about me owning a motorcycle, I guess because she thought I'd get hurt. Back then in California, you weren't required to wear a helmet and you didn't need insurance for a motorcycle so the only cost was for gas and maintenance. Since I made only about $25-$30 dollars a week part-time at the grocery store, I didn't have a lot of money, but gas was only 29 cents a gallon or less and food was pretty cheap, like 10 cents for a burger, 5 cents for fries, and 15 cents for a drink.

    People are always saying where there's a will, there's a way. I liked riding my motorcycle and I rode it to the beach a few times and went bodysurfing or did some homework while just relaxing on the beach. One day I thought, *why not take my 7' surfboard on the back of my motorcycle to the beach*? I've seen guys pulling a board behind a bike or moped around the beach area using a minitrailer. But I never saw anyone with a surfboard on a motorcycle on the road. I could let it hang behind me but I didn't think I could secure it so I decided to tie it right up the back along the tail. I wasn't going to go on the freeway because I was concerned about the possible crosswind because it can act like a wing if the wind catches it just right. And even without the board, the wind can push you around on a motorcycle. One day, the Santa Ana winds were kicking up with gusts of 50-60 mph. The Cahone pass going up over the mountains to Las Vegas would be closed to trailers, big 18-wheeler trucks, RVs, campers, and motorcycles. The winds have tipped them over in the past with strong gusts. One day, I was on the Santa Ana Freeway in the far left lane going about 70 mph when a strong gust pushed me over two lanes of traffic. I was lucky there were no cars there and that it didn't knock me over. I was pretty scared so I slowed down to about 50 mph and stayed in the far right lane after that. I didn't have any more problems with the wind but now I had to worry about cars running me over because I was going so slow. I made it home okay but I felt I was pretty lucky.

Santa Ana Winds—Beach Boys

Here in Southern California there is a weather condition known as the Santa Ana Winds.

Fire wind oh desert wind
She was born in a desert breeze
And wind her way
Through Canyon Way
From the desert to the silvery sea

In every direction
See the perfection
And see the San Gabriel Mountain scene

Santa Ana winds keep blowin' across my eyes
Santa Ana winds keep blowin' across my eyes . . .

Once I was able to get the surfboard secured, I figured I should take it for a test ride to make sure it would stay on and that I could handle it okay. I used a few towels and several stretch cords to hold it in place. I used the passenger foot pegs to help secure it and fastened it right up the left side of the backrest. It was pretty solid. Years later, I did a similar thing by putting my golf clubs and pull cart on the back of my motorcycle. I attached them on the seat laying flat right behind me using stretch cords. I did get some strange looks and some smiles and thumbs up.

When the day came to go to the beach, I loaded up the bike with some extra towels, my transistor radio, and food and other stuff in a bag behind me on the seat. I took the slower route so I wouldn't have to deal with the possible crosswinds, especially from trucks. The only part I was concerned about was the Brea Canyon pass going from Diamond Bar to Imperial Hwy because there are a lot of twists and turns and it can get windy there. So I just took it slow. Along the way, I noticed a lot of people checking out the board on the bike and got some thumbs up and other things.

I made it to Balsa Chica without a problem, parked the bike, unloaded everything else, and got the board waxed up and hit the waves. I only did this a couple of times more. It was awesome getting to the beach to go surfing anytime you wanted. But even better taking your board on a motorcycle. That was just an awesome time.

20

Over The Huntington Pier

(September of 1970)

Instrumental: Over the Wave—The Beach Boys

    In Southern California during the summer, the waves don't usually get too big. A big day is usually about 6-8'. But one day around early September in 1970, right at the end of the summer, some of the biggest waves I had ever seen came into Southern California. I happened to hear about this storm off the coast of Mexico and heard that some big waves would be hitting the shore. I could have gone to any of a number of places to surf but I wanted to go to a place I was familiar with and that had lifeguards still on duty. So I chose to go to Huntington Beach at the pier. This is where they usually hold all the surfing contests.
    The day before, a storm had formed a couple hundred miles off the coast of Mexico and had developed into a hurricane with winds of 100

mph or more. The storm never made land but it did produce some nice southerly waves which is perfect for anywhere below Santa Barbara. All up and down the coast from Northern Baja, San Diego, Cardiff-by-the-Sea, Laguna, Newport, Huntington, Long Beach, would get the best waves. Other places like Malibu, Leo Carillo, Redondo, would also benefit, but because of the angle, probably not the best shape.

***Instrumental: Stoked**—The Beach Boys*

David Nuuhiwa, Huntington Beach, 1966

Just about to wipeout. Gary Propper, Huntington Beach, 1965
photographs by Steve Wilkings

When I got there, I couldn't believe what I was seeing. The waves were breaking OVER the Huntington Pier which means the waves were up around 15-20'. I never saw waves break that far out. I heard that the pier was damaged by a storm a few years earlier and then rebuilt. They do a good job rebuilding the piers now because they seem to hold up a lot better to the storms. The next set was around 8-12' and the third set closer in was 6-8' with the shore break crashing right on the beach at 4-6'. You couldn't swim without fins because the current was so strong, so surfing was risky if you lost your board. The waves had great shape with nice long shoulders, the best I'd ever seen there.

The current was really strong, coming up from the south and the red flag was out due to the current conditions, which meant dangerous rip tides. To get out, you had to paddle at about a 45-degree angle towards the pier on the north side. You didn't want to go on the south side because the current would take you right into the pier. You could only get out to the second and third set of breaks because the white water from the first set was too big to get through and the waves were coming in too rapidly to paddle over them. It was tough enough to get out to the second set if you wanted to try those waves. You had to continuously paddle towards the pier while you waited for a wave, which didn't take long. Just as a wave was coming, you'd turn, drop in, jump up, and off you'd go. By the time you stood up, you were about one hundred feet up shore from where you started.

Instrumental: Theme from "Endless Summer"—The Sandals

The waves were really heavy and with my 9'2" Royal Hawaiian board, I could walk the nose, hang ten, even stand on the board backwards with the wave totally above my head. The waves were really fast and I must have gotten at least twenty or more really good rides, some tucked in tight in the curl. After a few waves, I'd go out to the second set and I was standing up in the curl. With the current that strong and with no leash, if you wiped out, you wanted to get to your board quickly. I was lucky this day and made nearly every wave and the ones I didn't make or didn't get out of clean, I got my board back quickly. After catching about five waves, you'd have to get to shore and walk a long way back to the pier because the current was so strong you couldn't possibly paddle back.

Still Surfin'—Beach Boys

He used to ride the sidewalks in a landlocked town
A solitary surfer still he got around
He had his favorite spots now
Where the best rides could be found

With posters on his wall from "Surfer" magazine
His room looked like a shrine to the surfin' scene
Go to Hawaii out of high school was his big time college dream
(That's where the girls are)

Did you ever wonder what happened to surfer Joe
He up and took a ride down to Mexico
With a pretty senorita we both used to know

You can see him catch a wave in the mornin' light
And sometimes you can find him on his board at night
A silhouette on water as the sun dips outta sight

He's still surfin (Still surfin')
He's still surfin' (Still surfin')

Surfers always love them summer days
With a board in the water rollin' with the waves
He's still surfin'

He's always been a surfer since the early days
Spendin' the summer searchin' for that perfect wave
He and his surfin' senorita never seem to age

In the mornin' light he's still surfin'
On his board at night he's still surfin'
In the summer days he's still surfin'
Rollin' with the waves he's still surfin'

SURFING ADVENTURES
of the '60s, '70s and beyond . . .

There were not a lot of us out there maybe eight or ten guys. No one could get out to the waves breaking over the pier except for the lifeguards. They were on the pier wearing life vests, jumping into the waves and bodysurfing these 15-20' monsters. I'd never seen anything like it. A couple of surfers wanted to drop in with their boards but the lifeguards wouldn't let them because they didn't want to have to make a rescue if they got wiped out and ended up in trouble. They had a blockade and had someone guarding the pier to keep people off of the pier.

I'm sure someone, somewhere was able to get out to the bigger waves that day but I never saw any one out there that far at Huntington. I never saw it that big again there but I'm sure in the following years, there have been other big days from other storms.

I Dreamed I was a Beach Boy, Too
James "Sunny Jim" White

When I was a boy in Texas
Heard the Beach Boys on the radio
Jan and Dean and that whole surfin' scene
And I just knew it was the way to go

Tucked that radio beneath my pillow
Those harmonies would filter through
Well I'd sleep through the sound of that music
I would dream I was a Beach Boy, too
I would dream I was a Beach Boy, too

I used to just dream of the ocean
Then I made it my reality
Now I live in a beach side town
My life of sweet harmony

I learned early that you've got to dream
Or you'll never have a dream come true
Now I play my guitar at all the beach side bars
Now I am a Beach Boy, too
'Cause I dreamed I was a Beach Boy, too

www.sunnyjim.com

A Time For the Sea and Me

A time has come in my life
To explore around in this world
Moving and traveling, searching for places to surf
Waves to ride and memories to find
Hoping—there is a time for the sea and me

Surfing makes me feel like
I want to stay here awhile
But when the time to go is here—I move on
Knowing I belong wherever I go feels so good
Because—there is a time for the sea and me

Just a picture is what I see
Although reality is what I feel
When I'm surfing I'm alive
I cherish the ocean and sea
For—there is a time for the sea and me

The only thing that I want
Is to be living near the ocean shore
The only place I'd like to be
Is surfing along the coast
Because—there is a time for the sea and me

Now when my time is up
I hope I will be near the shore
'Cause I love to feel the freshness of the sea
The waves, the ocean, the wind, my friends
And Finally—there'll be a time for the sea and me

Andy, 2/10/1972

21

internet open source

The Wedge

Instrumental: Balbao Blue—The Beach Boys

Most people have heard about "The Wedge" located in the southern most part of Balboa, California. It is south of Newport Beach and just north of Corona del Mar across the channel separated by two rows of rock jetties which was built to break up the waves so the boats could enter the Newport Harbor safely and to protect the boats during storms and large sea swells. "The Wedge" is on the north side of the channel and the waves that come in from the south whip around the jetty and just about double in size compared to the waves just up the beach a few hundred yards. In the movie *The Endless Summer* was featured "The Wedge" in one of the scenes. And yes, it does drop into about 1-2' of water. I've bodysurfed "The Wedge" with and without fins and its much safer with fins because you can get out of trouble faster but you'd better have fins that won't come off because I have two sets of fins at the bottom there along with hundreds or maybe even thousands of other peoples' fins. I suppose, on a calm day, you could dive down and salvage a whole lot of fins and resell them if you were so inclined.

photographs by Andy Forsyth
Small day at the Wedge, riding a boogie board.

I'm sure everyone who's bodysurfed at "The Wedge" has a story to tell. I went out one day when the waves were 4-5' and I didn't have any fins. After a couple of waves, I realized I was the only one out and the waves swelled to more like 8-10' or more. I couldn't get in because of the rip current and I couldn't get out because the waves came in too fast. I was stuck in between.

I've been in rip currents before and large waves 10-15' but when the waves are crashing right on the shore and I'm talking about maybe just a foot of water or less. You didn't want to try bodysurfing those waves. They were coming in fast and often. When the backwash went out, it took all the water with it and the waves just raised up 10-12' easily and came thundering right onto the shore.

SURFING ADVENTURES
of the '60s, '70s and beyond...

Several of us used to go to "The Wedge" to ride the waves, most of the time it was small to medium. This one time some guys from NY City were there. They had a VW "Flower Power" Van with NY plates and all their belongings stuffed inside, with surfboards on top. I guess they wanted to see what all the fuss was about this "Wedge" location. The waves were I'd guess 5-8' and breaking in 2 feet of water, straight down as usual. You'd get maybe a two-second ride. If you were lucky, you could get a ride to the left for 10-15 seconds but this is very rare. I've seen guys riding a boogey board and I even saw a guy stand up on the boogey board early in the morning when no one else was out and got a great ride through the tube and bailed out flying over the back of the wave just before it crashed. He did this several times before the bodysurfers started crowding in. Sometimes you'd see 10 or more guys take off at one time, bodies flying everywhere landing on each other. I personally never saw anyone get hurt bodysurfing at the bowl but maybe 50 yards north of the bowl I saw some people working on someone who had been bodysurfing the shore break and they were digging an air space in the sand around his mouth so he could breathe. Apparently, he must have hit his head and suffered a neck injury. Not long after, an ambulance crew showed up and got him onto a stretcher and took him to the hospital.

The guys from NY, after watching the way the waves were breaking, did not want to go out. With their NY accents, they made the comment, "Dat's nawt bawdy swerfin, dat's swuside." I agreed, but I went out anyway with my fins on.

Back to the big waves, I got stuck in. I didn't have any fins on and I was the only one still out. I somehow managed to swim through the current to get close enough to get my feet on the ground with about three feet of water ripping out. I couldn't hold my ground as the current took my feet out. I knew I was in trouble because a big 10-foot wave was building up quickly and was about to unload on me. I had to think quickly and I decided to dive for it so I went under the wave as low as I could and basically clawed the sand to keep low and get under the wave. I was lucky and made it deep enough so it couldn't lift me up ten feet and throw me onto the shore like a dishrag. I waited a few seconds for the wave to pass and I pushed up off the bottom and felt rubber, probably some fins. I wish I had them on my feet at that point. When I made the surface, I got as much air as I could and turned just in time to see another wave coming and just started swimming out. Someone later told me that when I was swimming out the wave was cresting and they could see my entire body and the wave was at least two and a half times my height. That would make the wave about fifteen feet since I am nearly six feet. It seemed like I was out there about twenty minutes but it was most likely only about four to five minutes. I was starting to get tired and I needed to do something quick. The waves farther north were crashing right on the beach so I could go there and to the south the waves were crashing on the rocks. I could swim out and try to make the rocks and then jump in the channel and swim past where the waves were breaking on the rocks and climb in. The problem there is that there are usually those giant jellyfish swimming near the rocks. After swimming out far enough, I finally made it to the rocks. Walked down and when the wave broke, I ran the rocks to get past the break. I made it safely to shore. Several of the people who were there in the water earlier came over to make sure I was okay. There are no lifeguards on duty at "The Wedge" so the swimmers are swimming at their own risk, just like the sign says. It also warns of possible dangerous currents.

 I just sat on the shore watching these large shore breakers, listening to their roar, and feeling the force of these huge waves as they crashed right on the shore. They were consistently 10-15'. I wish I had a movie camera or even a regular camera because it was quite a sight. I'm sure they've had large waves there but I'd never seen waves that big and I had only seen big waves like the ones at Waimae in the movies, so you couldn't really appreciate it or get a feel for what it was like. But this was real and if I hadn't made it to the rocks and instead tried to bodysurf the wave in, I don't think I'd have survived it. I watched enough of those things coming in and they were incredible. These waves were comparable to the ones that broke over the Huntington Pier. I would have liked to have seen those waves on that day at The Wedge.

22

painting by Bruno Turpin

Turn Left

We're heading for San Clemente today; it's early in the morning and Sefo is driving his parents' station wagon. There are only four of us going today: myself, Dave, Charlie, and Sefo. Dave's Helms truck is in the shop so Sefo was able to get his parents' car. Sefo is from Hawaii and is, by far, the best surfer. He's kinda short, around 5'7", and 180 lbs but very tough for his size and solid as a rock. He plays linebacker on the high school football team and doesn't take any crap from anyone. He's got two older brothers who are huge, like 6'2", or 6'3" and 280 lbs and they toss him around like a rag.

Sparky Hudson, San Clemente, 1966

Riding the nose. David Nuuhiwa, San Clemente, 1966

photographs by Steve Wilkings

SURFING ADVENTURES
of the '60s, '70s and beyond...

G.T.O.—Ronny and the Daytonas

Little G.T.O.
You're really lookin fine
Three deuces and a four speed
And a 389
Listen to her jackin' up now
Listen to her whine
Come on and turn it on
Wind it up blow it out G.T.O.

Gonna save all my money
And buy a G.T.O.
Get a helmet and a roll bar
And I'll be ready to go
Take it out to Pomona
And let 'em know
That I'm the coolest thing around
Little buddy gonna shut you down
When you turn it on wind it up
Blow it out G.T.O. . . . .

He was hoping to bring the Dodge "Super Bee" 440 cc big-block V8 that one of his brothers let him drive sometimes, but they were going somewhere with it. It is really loud. We didn't really believe him that it was that loud but as we were on the way to the beach on the Freeway we heard this loud roar coming down the road and Sefo starts freaking out, saying, "that's the Dodge, that's the Super Bee" and sure enough it was. It was so loud it didn't pass us for about twenty seconds on the other side of the freeway and we couldn't even hear our radio as it went by. It was a deep green, with yellow racing stripes, big slicks two huge barrels for exhaust pipes. You could feel the roar as we went by and could still hear it for a minute after we passed it.

When we finally got to San Clemente about 90 minutes after leaving we had to give directions to Sefo in town because he had never been there before. Well Sefo is a real character because he takes what you say literally. So we're driving along and Dave is telling him where to turn because he is in the front and when we get near this one intersection, Dave tells him to "turn Left up at the next street." Before Dave can say " . . . up at the next street" Sefo has made a left turn into someone's driveway and slams on the brakes. And we all just about end up in the front seat. Dave freaks out and Sefo is just as calm as can be and says "You told me to turn left". We are laughing hysterically and Charlie asks Sefo, "Why'd you stop for man? You could have cut across the yard and into the other driveway and back on the road." So what does Sefo do? He hits the gas, goes across the yard into the next driveway and back on the road. Well by now we are rolling and can hardly see straight. I'm sure those people weren't too happy when they saw the tire marks on their grass and the crushed flowers, but I'm sure it all grew back eventually. Good thing there were no cops around.

All we could talk about all day was "Turn Left," "Turn Right," "Stop," "Look Out." We rode it for all it was worth. Sefo was a good sport about it but after that Dave was much more careful about his directions, as we all were. In fact we used to be careful with directions even if Sefo wasn't driving just in case someone else decided to pull a "Sefo." So instead of "Turn Left at the next corner," it was "Up at the next corner, Turn Left." And then you had to hope he heard the first part. We learned to give directions at the end of the sentence instead of at the beginning. A whole lot safer with Sefo, but not nearly as much fun, that's for sure.

painting by Garry Birdsall

Ground Swell

SURFING ADVENTURES
of the '60s, '70s and beyond . . .

Summer Means Fun—Jan and Dean

Surfin' everyday down at Malibu
In the warm California Sun
No more books no more homework to do
Summer Means fun Summer means fun
Summer Means fun Summer means fun
The girls are two to one
Summer Means fun Summer means fun
Summer Means fun Summer means fun

Come on everybody get your baggies and bikinis
The party has just begun
We're gonna have a ball
I'm telling you all

Summer Means fun Summer means fun
And the girls are two to one . . .

23

painting by Bruno Turpin

Stop the Car

    Pete and I were driving along in an old Chevy Station wagon that his dad gave to him after he had put over 400 thousand miles on it. We were on our way to the beach but hadn't gotten out of town yet. A motorcycle was going by and I was checking it out but there also was a cute girl walking on the sidewalk and Pete was checking her out. Pete always would say that I would look at a motorcycle before I'd look at a girl, which I told him wasn't really true but actually I think it was true.

    As Pete was checking out the girl we were fast approaching another car that seemed to be slowing down. I alerted Pete that we'd better stop or we're going to hit the car. Pete hit the brakes and we were able to stop in time but Pete noticed that his brakes were pretty low. We pulled off the road and got a screwdriver and adjusted the brakes.

SURFING ADVENTURES
of the '60s, '70s and beyond...

We had a great day at the beach, the weather was great and the waves were really kicking. There were lots of girls in really small bikinis, which we liked. We went to San Clemente because there was usually better surfing there rather than at Huntington Beach. Besides Huntington Beach usually has more families and fewer beach bunnies. And the waves can be a little choppy, except near the pier and there it can get a little crowded. I got in some surfing in the morning and traded off using my 7' board and the 9'2" board trying to figure out which was better on these waves. Even though the 7' board was fun it was a little harder to catch a wave. I usually ended up doing most of my surfing with the bigger board.

Girls On The Beach—Beach Boys

On the beach you'll find them there
In the sun and salty air
The girls on the beach
Are all within reach
If you know what to do

How we love to lie around
Girls with tans of golden brown
The girls on the beach
Are all within reach
And one waits there for you
(Girls on the beach) . . .

Three different styles of surfing

Keith Paull and Russel Hughes, Hermosa Beach, 1970

Fletcher Sharp, Malibu, 1967

Mike Purpus, Santa Barbara Campus Point, 1968

photographs by Steve Wilkings

SURFING ADVENTURES
of the '60s, '70s and beyond . . .

In the early afternoon we were taking a rest and apparently I fell asleep and started snoring. Pete told me later that someone had commented about me snoring and asked, "Doesn't he sleep at night?" I think Pete told them something like "No he parties all night and sleeps during the day." Which is only partially true. I do like to party, but not all night, at least not during the week. When I woke up they were calling me party animal, Grizzly bear and some other funny things. I asked Pete about it later and that's when he told me about the snoring.

On the ride home we decided to go into Hollywood and ride down the Sunset strip. Since we weren't 21 yet and didn't have much money except enough for gas and food we couldn't do anything except drive around but it was pretty cool seeing all the wacky people, mostly hippies hanging around the street corners. There were also lots of hookers and we thought some of the hookers weren't really girls because they looked a little too masculine. To us that was just a little too weird. Good thing we didn't do that stuff because it was difficult to tell the difference with some of them. There were some normal looking people walking around too, probably some tourists sightseeing or people just out for a show, dinner or shopping. We were hoping to see some celebrities but I doubted we'd actually see anyone famous just walking around.

After a couple of hours or so we decided to head on home. The next day we were going to the gym to get in a workout in the afternoon so Pete came to pick me up around 2:00 PM. As we were heading to the gym Pete was having trouble again with the brakes and his foot was almost all the way to the floorboard. As we approached the next light Pete started to hit the brakes but the car wasn't stopping. He popped the car down to first gear and it slowed down the car but we were approaching an intersection and I told Pete "We need to stop this car." We were in the far right lane when Pete opened his door. At first I thought he was going to bail out but then he put his foot on the ground to try to stop the car. I would have put my foot out too but I didn't have my shoes on. Pete got it to slow down to about 4 mph and then on the right was a parking lot with a slight uphill incline so I told Pete and he immediately pulled into the lot and we slowed enough and he pulled the emergency brake. Good thing it worked. Wow that was close, I said "Pete, you tried to stop the car with your foot, you're a maniac, that was awesome." Then we started laughing because we both knew how close we had come to running into the intersection with all those cars flying by. He did slow it down enough but he also took a little rubber off his tennis shoes.

We weren't far from my house so I ran home to get my car. We got a tow truck for his car and got it to the auto shop to get his brakes fixed. Then we went to the gym to get in our workout. Well we did have a pretty good story to tell everyone at the gym and we all got a good laugh about Pete trying to stop the car with his foot just like the TV cartoon, "The Flintstones." Then a few of the guys began telling their own stories about their brakes giving out causing crashes and all kinds of other stuff. It got pretty outrageous with everyone coming up with something bigger and wilder. Pete picked up his car the next day. We were lucky, good thing we weren't going too fast and Pete had good tread on his shoes too. Some people aren't so lucky.

Onward Seagulls

Seagulls that play in the ocean spray
Are flying into the wind
Looking for sand crabs and clam meat
Or a handout from a stranger or a friend

Waves are crashing the sandy shore
The roar is a shield of protection
Against the ocean spray
The seagulls think it is a game

They dodge the waves
And dive for fish
Tease the surfers and fly around
They think the game is just for fun

Where once there was a lonely beach
And only the seagulls and sandpipers played
Are now hundreds of people's feet
And sounds other than squawks

Some of the seagulls move on
To other beaches
Where the ocean and sand await
The seagulls, the sandpipers and the surfers

Andy, 4/10/1973

24

photograph by Andy Forsyth

No School Today

Senior Ditch Day

In High School there was one day that was unofficially designated as senior ditch day, usually on a Friday in May, but it had to be a nice day to make it worth while. Each year I was in High School all or almost all of the seniors wouldn't show up for school on senior ditch day. It wasn't an official day off but "someone in" with the teachers, let them know we wouldn't be in and so the teachers would either call in sick or come in knowing we wouldn't be there and were ready to leave a little later. I think one year the teaching staff tried to stop them from taking off but the seniors still took off anyway.

Surfers Rule—Beach Boys

It's a genuine fact that the Surfers rule

It's plastered on the walls all around the school now
(Surfers rule, Surfers rule)
Becoming just as common as a golden rule now
(Surfers rule, Surfers rule)
Take it or leave it but you better believe it
Surfers rule

A Woody full of Surfers pullin' long side a wagon
(Surfers rule, Surfers rule)
The Hodaddies sittin' while the Surfers are draggin'
The Surfers are winnin' and they say as they're grinnin'

Surfers rule
(Four Seasons you better believe it) . . .

    I guess you could say it was a kind of self imposed holiday. The year we were seniors we went to Crystal Cove, near Laguna. It was an absolutely beautiful day. The temperature was perfect, in the mid 70s, the waves were perfect and even better because they don't impose the swimming area until June, so we had the waves for surfing all day.
    You couldn't have asked for a better day especially because there was hardly anyone out, the water wasn't too cold and almost no wind. And the best part was because we weren't in school today. In other parts of the country when it snows they will occasionally get a snow day and the kids get to engage in snow sports like snow boarding, snow skiing and for the unfortunate, snow shoveling first, before they can go out and play. So kids in warmer weather areas have to be a littler more creative in order to get a day off especially on really nice days.

SURFING ADVENTURES
of the '60s, '70s and beyond . . .

Anyone for Golf?

source PHS Yearbook, 1969

In my senior year we used to take off on Fridays once in awhile or leave early. One time a friend of mine and I took off to go golfing on a Friday. My uncle owned a 9-hole golf course in Claremont and he would let me play for free which was pretty cool. I always had the money but if he was on duty he never charged me. Unfortunately I wasn't a very good golfer at the time and shot about a 130 something for 18 holes. Bob wrote in my year book. "To Andy, a good friend, not a good golfer, Bob." In later years I improved quite a bit and even shot a four under par for 18 holes at my uncle's course for my best round there.

Orange Groves and Smudge Pots

On the last day of school before Christmas vacation about four of us, Leo, Eddie, Bill and myself cut school and got a case of beer. Although one of the guys, Eddie was only 16 he knew the guy at the liquor store and he got us a case of 16-ounce Colt 45 malt liquor. I think what he did was that the guy bought it and put the beer in the back of his car but left it unlocked. Then Eddie got the beer and left the money and locked the car. Then we had to find a place to go to drink the beer. It was about 10:00 AM by now and it was getting cold since it was late December. It can get cold in Pomona and the San Fernando Valley but it rarely snows. We got hail sometimes but almost never snow.

We went to an orange grove and found a place where some smudge pots were burning. The smudge pots are usually turned on when the temperature gets down to near freezing. They are usually positioned in the middle of four trees to keep the temperature warm enough to protect the trees. The smudge pots were nice and warm and we sat around drinking the beer and talking a lot, who knows what we were talking about, but we were having fun.

After a couple of hours we had just about polished off the beer and unbelievably it had started snowing. That just made it even better because we thought for sure they'd close the schools and let us off with a snow day. I guess that was really a stretch since it only snowed a couple of inches and had melted off by the end of the day.

Well to be honest I don't remember much of what happened after that. The guys drove me home and I'm not sure how they were able to drive but anyway they got me home. I closed the door and got my finger stuck in the door and broke it but I didn't feel a thing. To this day my finger is still a little crooked. When I got home I took off my shoes and one of my socks and walked over to the stairs and started hopping up the stairs on the foot with the sock. I wasn't talking too clearly from what my mom told me later and when I made it upstairs I just fell on my bed and went asleep. My brothers were asking my mom what was wrong with me and she just said he wasn't feeling well. She came up to check on me and found me lying there asleep and drunk. She called my dad who was at work because he was working the evening shift. My mom just told him that I had come home drunk. So during his lunch break my mom drove me to see him and I still wasn't real focused and kind of woozy. When he asked me what I was drinking I told him what it was and he just said "That'll do it." So then he asked me what we ought to do as punishment. I first told him that I'd never do this again because I didn't like the way it made me feel or act. Then I asked him "When you were my age did you ever get drunk?" I already knew he had so I kind of wanted to see what he'd say. And he just said "I think you've learned your lesson, just make sure this never happens again." Well I never got drunk like that again. Now that's not to say I didn't have a few drinks once in awhile but I was careful to make sure I didn't get that far gone ever again.

I guess it's kinda funny because when you're young and under the drinking age you can't wait to drink so you do it anyway, but then when you're legal the novelty wears off and you hardly drink at all anymore.

Stuck on the Mountain

Later that same year there was a group of about twenty kids in the Surf and Ski club that went up to Mt. Baldy to go skiing for the weekend and a big snow storm came in late Saturday and dropped eighteen inches overnight and they weren't able to get out and ended up stuck on the mountain until Tuesday because the roads were closed until they could get the trucks up there to clear the roads. The road leading up to Mt. Baldy is about twelve miles and is like a snake of winding roads and turns with some of the turns fairly steep. In some places there is a one hundred foot or more drop off. Even with railings it is dangerous in icy conditions. You had to have chains on your tires or you weren't allowed up or down. These twenty-some kids said they had a blast snow skiing. But when they got back they had a lot of homework to catch up with.

Baseball Day Off

I had a friend, Teddy, who was a big Pittsburgh Pirates fan and in 1960 Pittsburgh was playing the New York Yankees in the World Series. Back then the games were usually still played during the day even though most stadiums had lights. They still mostly played day games, especially for the World Series, so if you were in school you couldn't watch the game. Some kids brought in radios and I remember one kid had an ear plug and would listen during class until the teacher caught him. She took away the radio until after school was out.

In the East, games would start at 1:00 PM or 3:00 PM which would make it 10:00 AM or noon for us in the west. If someone had a radio we all gathered around and would listen during lunch and recess. We had one teacher who'd bring in a radio and play the game while we did our school work. But he'd tell us he'd turn it off if we weren't doing our work.

During the seventh game of the World Series Teddy somehow convinced his parents he was too sick to go to school and ended up watching the game on TV. When Bill Mazeroski hit the home run that won the game and the World Series for Pittsburgh he was so excited that he threw his shoe and accidentally hit the TV and cracked the screen. His parents were not too thrilled about that. When we saw him the next time he was telling us about what happened and we had a good laugh about it.

Something Simple

San Francisco with it's quaint houses,
Enormous office buildings,
And the Golden Gate Bridge,
Longs for something simple.

The New York subways rumble by
While skyscrapers test new heights.
The central park lights are dim,
And it too longs for something simple.

Orlando, Florida in the summer
Has the dream land of Disneyworld.
With it's fantasies of life
It is not really something simple.

Los Angeles has smog, the Dodgers,
And the freeways that border Disneyland.
Newport Beach tends to its' surfers,
Searching for something simple.

Chicago has world famous night clubs.
Old movies are made there
And tall sky scrapers that bend in the wind.
Chicago needs something simple.

Hawaii has summer all year long.
Honolulu is a city that is very popular,
Attracting surfers from all over the world.
But something simple is missing still.

Andy, 1/22/1975

25

drawing by Jane Forsyth

Full Moon Night Surfing

(Summer of 1968)

Part I, Day Surfing at San Clemente

As I'm sitting here trying to think about which story I want to write about next I'm gazing out the window and see a beautiful silver full moon lighting up the sky and everything else around. I can't help but think back to the first time I went night surfing. Back then we couldn't afford to stay in a motel so we either slept on the beach, which in Southern California was still legal in most areas except State Park Beaches. You had to be careful of high tide because you could get wet if you didn't stay far enough away from the tide.

On this summer day Pete and I went to the beach. Pete didn't surf but we worked out together lifting weights, running and training for football season. Pete was a big guy about 6'4" and 240 lbs. He tried using my 9'2"

Royal Hawaiian Surfboard once and could never manage to stand up so he just used my 8'6" Hobbie and used it like a big belly board so he had fun.

We went to San Clemente this time and it was a perfect day, good waves, not too crowded, lots of girls in bikinis and a good breeze now and then to cool you off. Most of the time I was in the water surfing and Pete was hanging around on the beach trying to get a girl to put suntan lotion on his back. Pete was a good guy but he was kind of pale and wanted to get tan, but he didn't want to get burned because he did burn easily even though he had olive colored skin. He wore glasses and had those thick Buddy Holly type rims. I first met Pete when we were in Boy Scouts together. We ended up in the same patrol and did a lot of camping out and hiking. In fact it was on a camping trip to the beach at Dana Point, before the jetty breakwater went in that I first saw someone surfing. A couple of scouts took their boards and went surfing during their free time or early in the morning. This is what got me interested in surfing.

San Clemente was a pretty good surfing area but the best waves were about a half mile south at the point. You could see some great waves breaking but you couldn't go down there because a certain person owned a house at that time by the name of Richard M. Nixon and they had the area fenced off. As you walked south towards the point there was a fence barrier and a sign that read "Restricted Area." It was about a half mile from the point. They also had a surfboard on the other side of the fence full of bullet holes. I guess it was their subtle way of saying "KEEP OUT!"

After surfing most of the morning I came in for a little rest. I laid down and almost immediately fell asleep. I guess I started snoring and got poked a couple times. I doubt it was that loud because there were a lot of radios playing and some were blasting music pretty loud. After about an hour I woke up and it was a little after noon. We decided to get something to eat. They had a hot dog and hamburger shack where we could get a cheeseburger for 40 cents, a soda for 25 cents, and fries for 15 cents. What a deal! Actually we thought it was kind of a lot since back at home the burgers were 20 cents. That was around 1968, I'm guessing. The bad part about surfing here is around 11 am they put up flags in the sand that restricts where the surfers can go. The best waves are right in front of the lifeguard stand where all the swimmers and booggie boarders are. We have to go down the beach a couple hundred yards. The waves aren't bad but they usually close out quickly and are smaller.

SURFING ADVENTURES
of the '60s, '70s and beyond . . .

Instrumental: Stoked—The Beach Boys

When the waves are 5-8' they are better usually with a nice left shoulder almost never a right. The waves where the swimmers are have a nice rights and lefts with a great shoulder. The afternoon picks up a little and we're getting some tough little waves 4-6'. They actually have a nice little curl to them. I'm eager to try out my new board but was waiting for some waves with some curl to them before trying it. I picked up a surfboard for $25 that was a used custom-made 7' board. It wasn't in bad shape, a few scrapes but no dings. I thought that these waves would be pretty good for this board. I had never been on a small board before. Most boards were 8' or longer, mine were 8'6" and 9'2". They had just started making the smaller boards a couple of years earlier. You'd see some guys with boards 5'10" or 6'6" and if you weighed more than 150 lbs you would be sitting on your board a few inches under water. Once you start paddling on your belly it surfaces so when you paddle to get a wave you can catch it. It's more maneuverable than the bigger boards but not easy to catch slower moving waves. With the bigger boards you can catch just about any size wave up to 10-15', but after that you really need like a 10' board or larger to go fast enough to catch the wave.

With my 7' board I'm just a couple inches in the water since I weighed around 160 lbs then. After lunch I might weigh 162. But all that surfing activity burns some off as well. Actually you don't even think about it because you're only about 17 anyway. Pete could not possible use my 7' board, not even as a belly board cause he'd sink about 2-3' under water and he didn't have the best balance on the big board anyway. He was a good football player, he played defensive tackle and running backs would run into him like a brick wall and just stop.

I paddled out on my belly because I can't knee paddle. Most guys like to knee paddle so they can see the waves better but I have knots on my knees so I can't knee paddle. I tried it before and it just hurt too much. Some guys develop surfer knots and it can be painful but mine were built in. I tried it once on my 9'2" board and after about thirty seconds I realized that I couldn't paddle this way so I just figured I'd paddle out on my belly. This presents another problem. When you wax your board you have to rough the wax a little by putting on a little sand so the sand on the wax is like sand paper scrapping off your skin (and nipples, ouch). So you have to learn to arch your back a little to keep your chest off the board so it doesn't rub on the board. The smaller board is easier to get through the waves because you can flip

211

over and push under the waves and pop out the other side, flip over and get out before the next wave breaks on top of you. Once you get past the break water you sit on the board and wait for the sets to come in. There's about seven to eight other guys out there and most of them are probably locals and are very familiar with where the waves will be breaking. You usually let them catch the first few waves to see how they're breaking before you try to finally catch a wave from a good set coming in and if you're in good position with no else around then you drop in, pop up, stand goofy foot, slide left, make a couple of cut backs stay close to the curl then slow down to let the curl catch up and get a nice cover up, then pick up speed a little climb the face and fly over the back of the wave just before it closes out. It was my first ride on my 7' board and it was a nice little ride. To my surprise a couple locals paddled over once I got back out and told me that was a pretty wicked ride. That made me feel pretty stoked and after that we'd talk and share other surfing locations and stories. They told me what it's been like here other days, especially big days when the storm waves come in, like in the winter. I also asked if anyone tried surfing the point and a couple guys said they had paddled down there and rode a few but the Secret Service comes around with shot guns and chases them out. A few years later after Nixon sold his property, the point was re-opened and it once again was a great surfing area. I never got to try it but it looked really good from where we were.

painting by Garry Birdsall

Reef Break

SURFING ADVENTURES
of the '60s, '70s and beyond...

Free As a Day and Night

A day is born, the sun is rising
Every land and place is filled with life
The air is silent and time is bringing
The soothing freshness at early light

The squawking seagulls and bristling wind
Fill the air each hour as they spin
Even the little sand crabs underground
Make the morning a very subtle sound

Running through the water for all to see
Are many young surfers as free as can be
Their grace like poetry is filling the sea
Their speed while surfing the waves so free

The sun is a morning start
For all to see, to love and be
A loud and deafening ocean roar
With waves crashing the sandy shore
As time passes, the day grows old
The sun is hot, the sand is warm
An evening moon against the sun's red gold
Are begging the surfers to stay some more

The evening stars are filled with color
As every surfer is gliding along
My ears can hear the ocean's roar
Of every wave crashing the shore

The moon is full, it's glow a silver light
While surfers ride in the moonlight
It's rays will fall to end the night
It lasts till then, and the early morning light

Andy, 3/19/1969

Part II—Night Surfing at San Clemente

So after a great day of surfing we drove around a little and hit another hamburger place to get some burgers, then we walked down to the San Clemente pier to check out the girls. I heard that a few years earlier a winter storm came in and did a lot of damage to the pier (maybe the same storm that hit the Huntington Pier?). So they had to rebuild it. I think it's held up pretty well since then. We hung out at the beach throwing the Frisbee around until we saw some guys getting ready to play football so we went over to see if we could join. We got picked on the same team and Pete played the line as usual and I was a receiver and defensive back. We had a lot of fun and our team won. I scored a couple of TDs. I found out that I was able to run pretty good in the sand when I was in scouts while we were camping at the beach and would play football on the beach.

After the game was over Pete and I hung around and watched the sun go down. The plan was to hang around so I could go surfing at night. It would be low tide and the waves were still good but the moon was overhead but wasn't bright enough yet because the sun had just set. It would be a couple of hours before it was dark enough for the moonlight to kick in. So Pete and I decided to go for a run. Even though we had just finished a football game we needed to get in some distance running. So we ran for an hour up and down the beach, doing some sprints too. We were both on the High School football team and were always working out to keep in shape. Pete loves to do sit ups so after our run he did a thousand sit ups, without stopping, I can only manage about 200 before I have to take a break because my abs start burning. Then Pete did another thousand. His upper torso was barrel shaped and solid as a rock. When we used to practice our hitting with a blocking dummy I couldn't even budge it when he was holding it and he would pretty much wipe me out. So I didn't like that drill too much.

Finally it was dark enough and the moon was going to be out for about three hours before the moon would drop off. The waves have an iridescent glow after they break, because of the moonlight, with the churning of the whitewater. It is really a beautiful sight and you could sit there all night just watching and listening to the waves. But the waves are out there just waiting to be ridden. So off I go into the water gliding over the first set of waves and dipping under the second set to get outside and wait for some waves to ride. Since I was the only one out there it is really cool but I basically just try to catch every wave I can unless it's too small. Even though it's medium tide the waves are doing pretty good. I'm getting some nice long rides. Pete's over at the lifeguard stand doing chin-ups while he's waiting for me to catch a wave. Sometimes he lifts up the lifeguard stand on two legs and uses it to do some curls like a weight lifter using weights. The guy is an animal.

The Surfer Moon—Beach Boys

There's a moon in the sky somewhere I know
Waiting for all the love to burn below
If you fall and it happens all to soon
Blame it all on the surfer moon

'Neath the hill 'hind the cloud one dreamy night
Rising up throwing down its golden light
If your heart hears this melancholy tune
Then you'll know it's the surfer moon

After a couple hours of surfing the moon is starting to get near the horizon and Pete is now sitting on the lifeguard stand just watching. As I catch a few more waves my silhouette travels through the glow of the moon. Pete says it was the coolest thing he'd ever seen. Which is pretty amazing because without his glasses he's legally blind, he can only see about ten feet. With his glasses he can see pretty good. He knows I won't be able to surf much longer so he comes down to the edge of the water and watches me catch a few more waves. He positions himself so that the moon is right behind me on the horizon. It would have been so cool to have a movie camera that could capture that. But back then it would have cost too much anyway and the lighting would be too poor. Now days a video camera could capture the images without a problem. At night the water is warmer than the air so you didn't want to come out of the water. Unfortunately after about three hours of surfing the moon goes down and it gets dark so I have to stop. Without the moon you can't see the waves anymore. It was a great experience and I couldn't wait to do it again.

Lucky Man—Scott Kirby

*I ain't on the airwaves
Right here by the blue waves
And only that crazy heron
Knows my songs
Fishes swim and birds they fly
I guess I'll sing until I die
The sunrise comes and goes
And I don't give a damn*

*But the moon is my spotlight
The surf is my band
The stars are my audience
On this stage made of sand
Some nights the loneliness
Is too hard to stand
But darling tonight
I'm a Lucky man*

http://www.scottkirby.com/

26

painting by Bruno Turpin

Shake Rock 'n' Roll

(May 1970)

    Some of the scariest things that happen don't necessarily happen on the water. On this particular day sometime in May of 1970, I was planning on going surfing before I had to go to work at 5:00 PM at the grocery store. At about 7:00 AM, I was suddenly awakened to a violent shaking and I fell out of bed, I tried to stand up but wasn't able to. I knew what was happening, it was an earthquake!!! I crawled over to the door and sat there and waited it out. I had felt earthquakes before but had never before felt one this strong. It must have lasted three to four minutes or least that's what it felt like. If I remember correctly it registered about a 6.9 on the Richter scale. There was a lot of damage done in and around the area.

My mom and dad came in to make sure we were alright.

> "Are you okay?" my mom asked.
> "Yea, was that an earthquake?" I responded, "Is the house ok?"
> She said, "Everything is fine just a few broken dishes, We'll have to check outside though."
> "That was a good one. It sure lasted a long time," I said.

We watched the news on TV after we checked out the house to find out what kind of damage had been done but everything around the house seemed ok. A few freeway overpasses had collapsed and even a new wing of a hospital collapsed or suffered some serious damage. There were also lots of buildings that suffered some damage as well and some scattered fires had broken out. I went to the store where I worked around noon to see what had happened to find that two of the four huge fourteen-foot glass windows had shattered. They were working to board it up until it could be replaced. I went inside to find merchandise all over the isles, broken jars, bottles, and even some of the refrigerated storage areas damaged and inoperative. People were working to clean up the mess and get things back to normal. I asked if I could help and they told me anything I could do would help so I pitched in and started putting things back on the shelf and cleaning up the mess.

Needless to say I didn't go surfing that day but from what I heard the waves were pretty awesome. I don't think they had any tsunami type waves but there were some larger than normal waves that day.

Traffic was pretty snarled because of the overpasses that collapsed and it messed things up for several months until they could get it all repaired. From what I've seen and read they construct the freeways and buildings now to protect against severe earthquakes so that it reduces the possibility of damage and collapses like these from occurring in the future. I remember the earthquake that occurred in San Francisco during the World Series in 1989 where a lot of freeways, bridges and buildings collapsed and there was widespread gas line ruptures and fires. That was pretty scary stuff and reminded me a lot of the one that hit Southern California. Earthquakes are so unpredictable. Even with all the seismic equipment to detect activity it is still a crapshoot to try and predict when one will occur. They have

SURFING ADVENTURES
of the '60s, '70s and beyond . . .

gotten better in recent years but it is still far from being an exact science. When people talk about part of California falling off into the ocean that is such a far stretch it is silly. Major continental changes takes thousands or millions of years to occur and happen so subtly that it is difficult to detect without sophisticated measuring equipment.

I used to work for NOAA, NGS which is the National Oceanic and Atmospheric Administration, National Geodetic Survey, located in the Washington DC area. We developed a computer database that would store information about the locations of geodetic location disks that were inserted into the ground and used to measure land movement and to create maps. There are disks all over the world that assist in monitoring shifts in the land and provide important data combined with other equipment like seismometers to help with the predictions of earthquakes.

Earthquakes and landslides can cause enormous waves like tsunamis or giant tsunamis but are very rare. There is a lake in the state of Washington where in the mid 1950s a land slide occurred that created 60-80 foot waves that traveled across the lake and wiped out trees along the way for about two miles to the ocean. There were four fishing boats on the lake that day and three fishing boats were destroyed but one survived with a father and son aboard and they talked about what happened.

The father said he heard this very loud noise and saw dust and water flying up that looked like a large bomb had been dropped. He said this huge wave was coming at them and he told his son to hold on tight to anything he could grab. The wave lifted them up and they rode the crest of this giant wave watching trees being wiped out until it made it to the ocean where they ended up being deposited. He didn't say what happened to the boat, if there was any damage but they survived and he reported the episode to the authorities but not much notice was taken except that the three other boats were lost along with their crew. He said no one investigated to see what had happened.

It was a miracle that they survived. The same thing happened again early in 2006 or 2007 but no one was injured on that one. This prompted some scientists and geologists to explore other parts of the world to see if something like this could have occurred in the past or could occur again.

During their studies and explorations they discovered an island off the coast of Africa that has an active volcano with the potential to partially collapse and fall into the ocean and create a 20' high swell with a two-mile wave length that would have enough water behind it to create a 200 foot wave or more once it reached the east coast of the US. With many lesser waves following behind it. This phenomenon was aired on the Science channel around October 2007.

These same scientists and geologists created some models to simulate the situation and measure the possible size and speed of the waves. They said about one trillion tons of debris could fall and slide into the ocean creating a giant tsunami wave.

The local government on this island along with scientists are taking steps to prevent this from occurring. They are doing this by artificially creating many small land slides and exploding dynamite in the hope of preventing a large land slide like the one they believed occurred several thousand years earlier. There are other islands with similar possible scenarios that are being studied very carefully. The potential damage of such a wave would basically wipe out everything on the east coast for up to eight miles inland. That is a very scary situation but with the technology available today scientists and geologists are able to identify these possible events and make recommendations as to how to prevent these from happening or minimizing the effect and potential damage.

Could you imagine someone trying to surf a 200 foot wave. I couldn't even imagine it. I doubt you could survive something like that. The 70 foot waves they are finding and surfing now are incredible. These 200 foot waves from what they said on the program travels about 500 miles per hour so it wouldn't be possible to catch them anyway. I would think they'd close out and just collapse and the wall of white water could be 70 to 80 feet or more it would be so destructive it would take down a building like it was a twig. If you'll recall the 15-20 foot waves that hit Sri Lanka in 2004 was incredible and that was a wave from an earthquake which are just waves the size of a normal hurricane. This would be ten times bigger. It is almost impossible to imagine something that big. Some of the movies created recently that portray a comet or meteor hitting the ocean and bringing in 80-100 foot waves are about as close as you could come to imagining what a wave like that could look like, just absolutely unreal.

Author's note to the reader:

That's pretty much it for the surfing stories. So I thought I'd toss in a few extra stories after this. The next couple chapters aren't about surfing but since I'd like to get more surfing stories maybe you'll see the kinds of stories I'm looking for. Maybe you know some famous people that you

SURFING ADVENTURES
of the '60s, '70s and beyond . . .

saw at the beach or that were surfing or some very unusual characters and you have a great story you'd like to share. I also included an excerpt from a surfing magazine that you should take a look at. Then I put in some surfing sites from around the world. Check out the web site for lots of great information about each site, what's around the area, lodging, etc. Oh yea, send me those stories! And stay stoked, surf's up.

Do It Again—Beach Boys

It's automatic when I
Talk with old friends
The conversation turns to
Girls we knew when their
Hair was soft and long and the
Beach was the place to go

Suntanned bodies and
Waves of sunshine the
California girls and a
Beautiful coastline
Warmed up weather
Let's get together and
Do it again

With a girl the lonely sea looks good [and bright]
Makes your nighttimes warm and out of sight

Well I've been thinking 'bout
All the places we've surfed and danced and
All the faces we've missed so let's get
Back together and do it again . . .

27

Interesting Characters and Famous People

Everyone has met one or more famous people. A guy that played on my softball team was an airplane pilot that flew for a private charter company and used to fly around lots of famous musicians, bands, celebrities, high profile athletes, etc. So this is just a list of some famous people I've met along the way or interesting characters I've met or known. But only one famous surfer of note. I went to a few surfing contests but didn't meet any of them by going up and talking to them. The only famous surfer I've ever met and talked with was Jeff Clark of Mavericks and Half Moon Bay.

Jeff Clark, Big Wave Surfer, Mavericks

In August of 2007, I took a trip to San Mateo in Northern California to spend a long weekend with my fiancee, Marilyn, while she was on a business trip. On one of my free days I drove over to Half Moon bay to visit the surf location known as Mavericks at Pillar Point. I had heard about it but it wasn't until I saw the movie "Riding Giants" that I knew more about this unique place or even where it was located. While at Pier 39 I bought the movies "Mavericks," "100 Ft. Wednesday," and "Condition Black." It was really a treat to be where Jeff Clark walked to get to the place where he surfed for fifteen years alone before anyone else would surf with him. It is also the place where Mark Foo, big wave surfing legend, lost his life in December 1994. After walking around some, and taking some pictures, I decided to stop by the Maverick's Surf shop, which is owned by Jeff Clark. I didn't really expect to see him but when I pulled up there he was in the parking lot talking with one of his employees. I got out of the rental car and just said "Hi Jeff." He said "Hi" back. I got out the "Riding Giants" and "Mavericks" DVDs and asked if he would sign them. He was getting ready to go into San Mateo to do some business but he took the time to sign the DVDs and talked to me awhile while he was running around his trailer and surf shop. I wish I had gotten a picture. I did get some pictures of his surf shop. Seems like I always forget to get pictures. Oh well. I told him that I was writing a book about my surfing adventures and he said he also was writing a book about some of the places he'd been surfing the big waves and the trips they took. He also showed me a bottle of beer that was being brewed under the "Mavericks" label. Can't wait to sample it.

It was a great honor and thrill to meet him. He is a very genuine and approachable person and I appreciate him taking the time to talk with me. Here I am a 56-year-old getting an autograph from a 40-something surfing legend. That has to be one of the highlights of my surfing encounters. I used to watch the surfing contests at Huntington Beach and would see all the surfing greats, top notch surfers, but that doesn't even compare to meeting Jeff Clark. Thanks Jeff.

Buddy Ebsen

The most famous person I ever saw at the beach was the actor Buddy Ebsen. You'll recall his famous TV roll as Jedd Clampett in the old 60s TV comedy series *The Beverly Hillbillies*. We were at Leo Carillo State beach on our family vacation and it was the year before I started surfing. I used to watch the guys riding the waves and I kind of knew that I'd be out there one day. Little did I know that it would be the next year. I think the year was about 1965 when we were there probably in late July or early August. On this day we were at the swimmers side where they have a life guard, this is the same location where Burt Lancaster and Deborah Kerr were rolling on the beach in the movie "From Here to Eternity." The setting for the movie was Hawaii but this scene and many others were filmed at Leo Carillo State Beach.

We were just hanging around the beach playing in the sand or doing what we usually do. Then Buddy Ebsen comes down the steps with a lady friend. We asked our mom if the woman was his wife, but she thought the lady was his secretary. She was much younger than he was. After a while he got up to go swimming. Now he was kind of skinny, with skinny legs and not much of a bottom. When he was swimming a wave hit him and the next thing we saw was that he was standing there with his back to the beach and his trunks around his ankles. He quickly pulled them up and tied them a little tighter. We were laughing harder than we ever did. All my brothers and my mom and dad all saw what had just happened. There was Jedd Clampett standing there naked, it wasn't a pretty sight but it was funny. We couldn't stop talking about it. Later that day we were walking back past where there are some outdoor showers, I think about four of them outside the restrooms. Buddy was showering at one of them and my mom went over to take a shower next to Buddy Ebsen. I should have taken their picture but I didn't have the camera. That would have been a sight, fortunately his swim trunks held up during the shower.

Rodney Forsyth, my grandfather

He was a really cool guy and great person. He raised three daughters and one son, my father. When he was around 60, he had to have a pacemaker attached to his heart to keep it beating properly. When I was in my late teens I would sometimes drop in on him unexpectedly and we'd talk or he'd help me with my bicycle that I was turning into a chopper style bike.

Once after coming back from a day of surfing with my surfing buddy, Charlie, he was working on his car and listening to the baseball game on his portable transistor radio. He loved listening to the Dodgers. He had a radio in the garage hooked up with speakers so he could listen to the game while he was tinkering on something in the garage.

I introduced Charlie to my grandfather. As I said, he was working on his car. He told us to watch this. And he tuned the radio to another frequency and held the radio next to his pacemaker and then put his other hand on the carburetor to his car while it was running and you could hear a tick-tick-tick noise. Then he adjusted the car and the ticking got faster. Then another adjustment and it slowed down. He was using his pacemaker to tune his car!!!

We thought that was great. Now, I hope he didn't do that a lot, but he did go through three pacemakers in eight years before he finally died of kidney failure just a few days before Christmas in 1972.

Edmund Shumpert

Ultimate Challenge surfing sculpture as it appears in Huntington Beach.
Internet open source

An example of one of his Surfing Trophies.
Internet open source

SURFING ADVENTURES
of the '60s, '70s and beyond . . .

You already know about Edmund, the sculptor and artist who lived at Cardiff-by-the-Sea. We camped on the empty lot next to his house. I saw examples of both of these sculptures as he was working on them in his shop. He also had a large marble block of stone that he was working on. I don't recall what he said it was going to be.

Shumpert studied at the prestigious Art Center School in Los Angeles and spent four years as a medical illustrator at the Brain Research Institute at UCLA. There he studied muscle structure to familiarize himself with the human anatomy in preparation for his profession as a sculptor.

The effort paid off and today he has become an expert of sorts on sculpting subjects with an athletic theme.

Among his subjects in the past were Johnny Weissmuller, the two-time Olympic swimming champion who later played Tarzan in 12 movies, and Olympic swimmer and gold medal winner and surfer Duke Kahanamoku.

Shumpert has sculpted native Americans including Sitting Bull and a bronze surfing scene that is now a landmark on California's Huntington Beach.

Shumpert's current project is another water scene that will be erected along the East Coast in Maryland.

Steve Smith

Norm was invited to a BBQ at a guys house in LaVerne, Calif. His name was Steve Smith at least I think it was Smith. He and his family lived in an old two-story house. He was the singer and song writer in a band. He wrote the 60s hit song "Don't Let the Sun Catch You Crying." Unfortunately he sold the rights to the song because at the time he needed the money. He didn't even get credit for writing the song. He had some unusual cats, a couple of dogs, some snakes, an iguana, a ferret and a red fox as pets. The cats were the ones with six toes, polydactyls, like the ones at the Hemingway House in Key West, Florida. He had a Golden Afghan and a Llahsa Apso. I only saw the red fox once as it darted across the room and made a quick left turn on a dime and scooted under the couch to hide. You could see it under the couch but it wouldn't move. I guess it didn't like all the people. There were about a dozen people there mostly friends of his. My friend Norm ran into him at a club and he invited him to his house for the BBQ and he asked if he could bring along a couple of friends. His band was pretty good because they played in a lot of local clubs and did some traveling around from what they told me. Don't know what became of them but every time I hear the song on the radio I think of him and that fox. He was an interesting guy, kind of a free spirit but very friendly.

Marty Hogan, Racquetball Professional

Marty is the former six-time number one professional racquetball player during the 80s. He single handedly changed the way racquetball was played using power, control and speed to overcome finesse, touch and guile by the older more established players. I first met Marty at a racquetball Pro Stop tournament in 1983 at the Merrit Security Racquetball Club in Baltimore, MD. Then three years later the manager of our club asked me if I'd like to play racquetball with Marty Hogan while they were filming an infomercial promoting eye protection.

So for two afternoons, I played racquetball with Marty, did some different scenes where I had to re-enact a set up shot as though I was about to hit him in the eye with the ball. I then had to go check on him after I hit him. It was a great experience meeting him and talking with him between takes. He was a real down to earth guy and one of the best racquetball players ever, sort of like the "Babe Ruth" of racquetball. The only thing I got was a video of the infomercial, which also featured a prominent player of the Utah Jazz at the time, Thurl Bailey, as the commentator for the infomercial. He had suffered an eye injury and now wore protective eyewear much like Kareem Abdul-Jaabar wore. The video was distributed to college, clubs and shown at racquetball clinics during the push to get people to wear approved racquetball eye protection.

Reuben Gonzalez, Racquetball Professional

Then there's Reuben, what can I say about him. Like Marty he too is a former number one professional racquetball player, but achieved the feat at 39 years old. The oldest ever to end the season at number one. I first saw him play in 1984 at the Merrit Club in Baltimore, MD, playing in the OPEN (Semi-Pro) division. He was like a cat, the way he moved around the court. He was only a year younger than me but was very good. He didn't start playing until he was in his late 20s. He was a National Champion one-wall handball player for a few years before switching to racquetball.

During an interview in the National Racquetball Magazine he was asked what would have happened if you had been playing racquetball earlier, how do you think you'd do against Marty Hogan and the others? His answer was, "There wouldn't have been a Marty Hogan."

In a tournament the year before he become number one he was playing against Marty in the finals of a Pro Stop tournament in Crystal City, VA and was serving for the match and the championship point. During the rally he hit a shot that would have ended the match and the referee called it good. Marty challenged the shot but the call stood up. Reuben was walking out towards Marty as though he was going to shake his hand but instead he gave the ball to Marty and said "It skipped." Reuben knew it skipped but wanted to see what the referees decision was going to be before he overturned it.

That is so rare in a sport of any kind, especially tennis, baseball and other sports where even if you know a call is bad, you go with what the referee calls. Marty went on to serve and won the match and tournament.

The place gave Reuben a standing ovation after the match and Racquetball Honored him later in the year with Sportsman of the Year. It would have been his first pro win. Next year he came back to win several tournaments and finished number one.

Over the years, I ran into Reuben several times and talked to him about racquetball. I knew one day I'd get to play him. Then in May 2006 in Houston, Texas, during the National Championships I would get the chance to play Reuben if I won my first match. I did win and got to play Reuben. I got my picture with him and some footage of the match. We were playing in the 50+ OPEN division. I was ahead in both games we played but ended up losing. He won both the 45+ and 50+ Divisions without losing a game.

At the Racquetball Awards Banquet on Saturday evening he was inducted into the Racquetball Hall of Fame for his achievements and contributions to the game of Racquetball. He still plays on the pro tour and is in the top 20 consistently. He recently has done some abstract racquetball paintings that he sells at the tournaments and online.

Charlene Tilton

I was in Carmel, California on a business trip one year. In the morning I would run the beach then go for a swim and do some bodysurfing each day. My brother drove over one day to visit and we went to dinner at Clint Eastwood's restaurant the "Hogs Breath." While we were eating diner there was some commotion going on at the front entrance. At first we though maybe Clint was coming in but it wasn't him it was Charlene Tilton of the TV drama show "Dallas." She was there with her new husband and a bunch of their friends or her entourage. This was during the time when the show was in it's second or third year, I'm guessing around 1984. Anyway I could see her from a distance but I didn't go over to get a closer look.

Other famous people I've met or have seen in person

Gene Shue—Washington Bullets Basketball Coach and former pro Basketball Player.

> I played racquetball with him several times

Craig Laughlin—Washington Capitals Hockey player and Home Team Sports Cable TV analyst.

> I played racquetball with him also and ran into him a couple of times at a local video store in Crofton, Md.

Cal Ripken—Baltimore Orioles Hall of Famer.

> Shook his hand at Camden Yards, and got an autograph, but who doesn't have his autograph, he would stay after the games for hours signing autographs for the fans.

Boog Powell—Baltimore Orioles Hall of Famer Baseball Player.

> Met him three times at Oriole Park, Camden Yards, Baltimore at Boogs BBQ Stand. First time I talked to him for fifteen minutes, at his BBQ stand when no one else was around. Got his autograph each time on my ticket.

Pete Seeger—Folk Singer.

> Signed his book for me, shook his hand, and got to talk to him for a couple of minutes. I wish I had a couple of weeks or more to talk and pick his brain.
> This was at his book signing at a book store around Thomas Circle, Washington, D.C.

SURFING ADVENTURES
of the '60s, '70s and beyond . . .

Loretta Swit—Actress

> At Disneyworld around 1992 at the Whoopdeedoo Review we were about two tables away from her with her mother.

Richard Bull—Actor, Little House on the Prairie, played the part of Mr. Olson.

> Met him at Knotts Berry Farm, Anaheim, Calif. He was at a booth waiting for people to talk to him. There was another actor in another booth with a lot of people around but no one was at Mr. Bull's booth. My wife and I went over to talk to him and she ended up talking to him for over 45 minutes while I did some looking around. She had always admired his acting over the years. She was a movie buff and appreciated the lesser known actors and actresses.

Wes Unseld—Washington Bullets player in the 80s, later he became coach of the Washington Wizards and Vice President.

> Shook hands with him and chatted for a minute at their summer practice facility when he was a player.

Manute Bol—Washington Bullets player 7'7" tall.

> Shook hands with him the first day he was in Washington at their summer practice facility.

Brad Cuseno—College Football player in the 70s

> Played racquetball with him several times when he came down to Maryland to visit. He was a friend of my racquetball buddy Jim Louwsma, they both went to the University of Miami, Ohio together and played on the football team there. Brad is the answer on two of the sports questions in the popular board game "Trivial Pursuit" for his achievements in the Bowl game that led to their national Championship.

28

photograph by Jane Forsyth

Absolutely Nothing to do with Surfing

Football, New Years Day

As kids growing up like all kids we'd like to play and have fun. We'd play kick the can, kick ball, capture the flag, steal the stick, hide and seek. We'd also ride our bikes, go swimming during the summer at the public pools and as we got older we'd play baseball, basketball, tennis, ping-pong (we had a table in our back yard), soccer, skateboarding, and football. For skateboarding we took our old clip on roller skates and pull them apart and nail them to a board and that was our skateboard. Besides skateboarding I think baseball and football were our favorite things to do. We'd get about six, seven, or eight of the kids in our neighborhood together for some games (Kenny, Teddy, Dan, Paul, Alan, Chris, Brad, Mike, Andy, Guy). And sometimes we'd even challenge other neighborhoods against kids our same age. Usually about eight to twelve years old. When I was around seven or eight, I remember playing against these big High School kids.

We'd have fun and they were good sports and let us play and even threw a pass to us sometimes.

Our favorite day to play football was on New Years Day. We'd play in the front or back yard of one of our houses. We'd pretend we were in the Rose Bowl or one of the other bowl games like the "Orange Bowl," the "Sugar Bowl," the "Liberty Bowl" or "Fiesta Bowl." We had a great name for our backyard football games on New Years day. We called it appropriately, the "Toilet Bowl." My brothers, Chris and Mike played on some Pop Warner teams. They were both quarterbacks on their teams. Chris's team was invited to play at a place where the stadium was called the "Chili Bowl." They had great chili and it was really cool seeing him play in a bowl game even though it was just a Pop Warner game. At least it was bigger than our back yard. We had a lot of fun at our back yard "Toilet Bowl" Games, there weren't any adults or referees around and we would pretend we were our favorite star quarterback or receiver. Baseball games were the same. No adults or umpires, just us kids having fun.

Up to Mt Baldy on a Motorcycle

There's really nothing special about riding a motorcycle up the road leading up to Mt Baldy on a summer day. I've been up there many times over the years by car, motorcycle, jeep, etc. It's a very steep climb and can be quite treacherous in the snow. Rocks fall onto the roadway so you have to "Watch for Falling Rocks" as the signs read. We always wondered which Indian was named "Falling Rocks" and why our dad told us we had to watch for him but that's another story. There are a couple of tunnels that were cut through the mountain where its fun to honk your horn and hear it echo through the tunnel. I even took my movie camera one time and filmed a lot of the ride up and down the mountain, especially the scenic overlooks and going through the tunnel.

I guess it was sometime during the summer of 1971 when I drove my motorcycle all the way up to the ski lift area parking lot. While I was up there I had this idea that I wanted to go down the mountain by just coasting with the engine off. Once I got past the town of Mt Baldy it was all downhill, with a few long straight stretches, but mostly there are lots of curves. I shut off the engine and for the next ten to twelve miles I just coasted. I had to apply the brakes on the sharp turns but I would pick up speed pretty quickly.

It was the coolest sensation riding down the mountain with no sound just the wind. Sort of like being in a glider airplane or SURFING. I usually got around 40 miles per gallon but when I checked it the next time it was over 50 mpg. I always wanted to do it again but never did. There was only one part for about 400 yards or so where it went uphill a little and I thought I'd have to start the engine but I made it over and started down hill again. There are lots of scenic over looks along the way where you can stop to take pictures. And there's the San Gabriel State park where you can go hiking as well. Over the years I've stopped at probably all the overlooks and hiked many times around the San Gabriel State Park with my sons on visits out there.

Fishing at Lake Arrowhead

Pete and I used to go fishing sometimes at Lake Arrowhead. I think I may have caught only about a half dozen fish over the four summers or so that we were going up there. We probably went four to five times a year each summer. Pete was a pretty good fisherman. I think he would catch several fish each time. I guess they didn't like my worms. At least I learned how to untangle a fishing line; many times over. One time we took a small boat up with us and onto the lake and I had this vision of the boat capsizing because Pete was a lot bigger than I was by about 80 lbs. I wasn't really worried because I was a good swimmer but I wasn't too sure about Pete. Good thing we had life vests.

Pete set up two lines and after a half hour or so he got a bite on one and started pulling it in. I had my hands full with my line and was bringing in one of my rare catches when his other line starts quivering. He tries to put down his first rod and grab the other and the fish lunges and there goes his rod in the water, gone! I'm in hysterics and I'm remembering Pete sticking his foot out to try to stop the car and I'm thinking he's going to jump in to save the rod!!! But he doesn't. He was really pissed because that rod was fairly new. To make it worse the fish on his other line gets away. So he had to bait another hook and he's mumbling to himself then after awhile he starts getting a nibble again. After a couple of good quick jerks he gets it hooked. He reels in the fish after a few minutes and while pulling it in he notices another hook in the fish's mouth and I'll be darned if there isn't a line on the hook and Pete starts pulling in the line and out pops his other fishing rod. Now how lucky was that. Pete was very excited and I thought we were going to capsize he was jumping around so much. I bet that doesn't happen every day.

First Airplane Flight

A guy I worked with at the grocery store for a few months, Mike, I had gone with him on his Catamaran sailing sometimes also knew I went surfing and liked to go to the beach. I tried to get him to go surfing but could never talk him into it.

Turns out he is also taking lessons towards becoming a pilot. He is certified to go solo and needed to get in some hours so he asked if I'd like to go up with him. I was about 19 at the time and he was only 18. I had never been in an airplane before and this was a two seated, one propeller plane that belonged to his uncle. After he checked in and set up a flight plan we got in and took off. We were flying around for a while when he asked if I'd like to take the controls.

Hey Andy, "Do you want to fly the plane?"
"Sure," I said, "What do I do?"
"You just steer it like a car but don't make any sudden turns."
"Pull the steering wheel to go up and push it in to go down"
"Great," I said, "This is really cool"

So for about fifteen minutes, I was flying the plane. The first time I was in a plane I was flying it!!! How awesome was that. We saw a fire over in the vicinity of Redlands so we got clearance to deviate from our flight plan to check out the fire, but we were advised to keep a safe distance in case there were any fire control planes that may be in the area. We kept our distance and headed back after checking it out. It wasn't a big fire just a brush fire covering about a couple of acres and it looked like a few trees were on fire as well but it wasn't near any houses.

It was really cool flying around in the local area. Places I knew from the ground looked a lot different up there. I always thought it would be great to be able to fly a plane but that was the only time I ever flew a plane. I've been in lots of commercial planes, large and small but I'll always remember my first plane flight, because I got to fly the plane. I guess you could say that was my fifteen minutes of fame and glory.

Catamaran

The same guy that took me on my first airplane flight, Mike, also had a catamaran. We went to Newport Harbor where we took it to the public slip. We lifted it in the water and we set out for the afternoon. There was a good breeze and being on a catamaran you could get up some pretty good speed.

On the way out we saw a huge yacht docked in the Newport Harbor. Mike told me it was John Wayne's yacht and he said that he heard it cost about $10,000 a day to run, with the cost of the fuel and the crew that he needed to run it. And that was in 1970. It was huge I'd guess about 130 to 140 feet long at least.

We stayed out several hours and we got going pretty fast and very nearly tipped it over a couple of times but were able to hold on. When we were getting ready to go back the wind was starting to die down a little. We could go in through the harbor channel between Corona Del Mar and The Wedge or go over the waves a few hundred yards north of The Wedge and land on the beach and carry it to the road about 60 to 70 yards and then go get the car. It wasn't that heavy but we were a little concerned about the size of the waves so we decided to go around. It took four hours of tacking back and forth to finally get to the landing.

Rolling down the Sand Dunes

After riding a jeep over the sand dunes at San Louis Obispo at the Oceano Dunes State Vehicular Recreational Area for an hour or so we thought it would be fun to roll or summersault down the sand dunes. Several of us were rolling sideways which was fun but you had a hard time going straight and got pretty dizzy. Then we started somersaulting. You could go faster and wouldn't get as dizzy. There was just one little minor problem, it was difficult to figure out when to STOP after about eight or ten rolls. It definitely gave you a big headache when you were somersaulting and landed about twelve inches into the sand with your head. You'd come out with your hair full of sand, ears and mouth full of sand, a sore neck and giant headache. You're lucky that you didn't break your neck. More than one of us had that problem, you'd think we would've learned. The next day you woke up with a nice migraine headache and a sore neck, but being young you don't let it stop you from enjoying yourself anyway. We'd go out riding the dunes again the next day but no sand dune tumbling this time.

After a Basketball Game

I mentioned in an earlier chapter that I used to play on our church basketball teams. I was even the coach of the Junior High team right before I went in the service. I played on the Junior High and High School teams when I was younger and we were pretty good and even won a couple of league championships. I took over coaching the Junior High team after about five games into the season when the other coach was moving out of town. Two of my brothers, Brad and Mike were on the team and the team was 5-0 when I took over. They ended up going undefeated and won the league championship.

I played on the adult church league basketball team in 1970 and 1971. Our minister was also on the team, he played point guard and he wasn't bad. I played power forward and was a pretty good rebounder and could actually dunk, but I only did it once in a game. I was going for a loose ball one time and ended up going head first into the padded wall. Thank goodness it was padded. But still I was kind of dazed and confused the rest of the night even though I kept playing.

On the way home I was feeling a little light headed and may have been weaving a little because a policeman pulled me over. He asked if I'd been drinking and I said no. He also wanted to know what that smell was. I told him I had just finished playing basketball and I hadn't showered and that the smell was me because I was still sweaty. I told him what happened when I ran into the wall. He said I probably shouldn't be driving. He gave me a field sobriety test anyway which I passed. But I needed to eat something because I hadn't eaten in awhile and I was still a little woozy.

When I got home my family had just finished eating home prepared tacos, which I really enjoy. All the fixin's were still out and so I cooked up the four remaining tacos in the package. After I finished them off there was another package of a dozen shells which after about a half hour they were gone too. I guess I was hungry. My mom came in to clean up and asked where the unopened pack of tacos was and I told her I was hungry and ate them. She just laughed, shook her head and said, "I guess you were."

Three Months of Freedom Left

My draft number was 150, by May of 1971 they were up to about 130 so I knew it wouldn't be long before I'd be drafted. I looked into the Air Force, Navy and the Army. I don't really know why I picked the Army but I enlisted in June of 1971 for three years in an MOS that would give me a good chance of going to Europe rather than Vietnam. I entered the delayed entry program so I wouldn't actually have to go in until September so that gave me three months of freedom before the Army would get me. I did lots of surfing, traveling around on my motorcycle and just enjoying my last days of freedom. It was during this time that I took Jay and my girl friend, Carrie, to the beach in July just before Jay went into the Army. Remember I ran into him at Ft Monmouth, New Jersey in November of 1971.

With two weeks left I went on a trip for about seven days up the coast on my motorcycle. I went up Highway 1 and stopped for the night at Leo Carillo and watched the guys surfing knowing it would be a long time until I'd be surfing again. I did go over there the weekend before I went in to get in my last rides. It was two years before I'd surf again.

I spent the night at Leo Carillo and then the next day I drove up the coast towards San Francisco and made lots of stops along the way to watch the surf and see places I'd never seen before. I drove around Big Sur a little. What a beautiful area that is. Someday I'd like to go back there again. Somewhere along the coast past Big Sur I saw some pretty good sized waves maybe 10-15' breaking about a half mile offshore. It could have been a place called "The Ranch," at the time I didn't even know exactly where it was but I stopped for about an hour to watch. No one was surfing there but they were definitely some nice surfable waves. As it got dark I stopped at a camping site somewhere and found an empty camping lot and crashed for the night. In the morning I got up early and headed out.

I went past Monterey and got something to eat and walked along the shore a little. Later that day I made it up to San Francisco and drove around. I followed the Scenic Drive Route for a little while. I made it up to the twin peaks and could see all of San Francisco, Oakland, Alcatraz and the Golden Gate Bridge. Then I drove over to go down Lombard Street, the steepest street in San Francisco. As I was getting ready to go over the Golden Gate Bridge my odometer cable snapped and so I had to find a bike shop and replace the cable. On the way to the shop my helmet fell off my bike. I wasn't wearing it around the city because I wanted a better view.

SURFING ADVENTURES
of the '60s, '70s and beyond . . .

The helmet rolled about 50 yards before it stopped and I couldn't find the plastic visor that snaps on so I went the rest of the trip without it.

I went over the Golden Gate Bridge then came back again and went over to Candlestick Park, the baseball stadium. It looked like they were doing some work on it so I drove over to the entrance. It was open and so I drove through the halls of Candlestick Park on my motorcycle. I probably shouldn't have but how often do you get a chance to ride a motorcycle through a baseball stadium. I made it out without anyone chasing me or calling the cops so I figured I better get going. I went over the Golden Gate Bridge again and up to Sausalito. I guess I was a little low on oil because it stalled out on me and when I checked the oil there wasn't much. A couple of guys on motorcycles offered to give me a tow to a gas station about a mile away but I was able to get it going ok but couldn't go very fast. I followed them and they put in some oil and filled me up with gas and they didn't even charge me for the oil or gas.

Along the way on the trip when I'd stop at fast food places they would ask if I was on a trip and when I told them I was and was from the LA area they would give me a burger, fries and a soda without even charging me. Which was really cool. In fact most of the time I didn't even pay for gas because people would know I was on a trip and it would cost like 75 cents to fill up and they would tell me it was covered. On the entire trip I spent a total of $13 and $6 of that was for the odometer cable.

I drove up to Oregon and then over to the Redwoods and slept in a state park sometimes or along the side of the rode where a bunch of 18-wheel trucks were parked. I was so tired once that I just slept on the pavement next to my motorcycle where a bunch of trucks were parked. I could have been run over by a truck if they didn't see me there.

On the last day I came down Interstate 5 and through the Grapevine. I went all the way without turning off the motor, because I had a hard time starting it the last time. I only had to fill up three times. I got some food to eat but drove straight through for the most part.

Going through the Grapevine it must have been migrating season for the butterflies because there were millions of them out. It was almost like a snowstorm there were so many of them. So for the next twenty to thirty miles I was splattered with butterflies. I had no plastic visor so I got a lot of them on my face. When I finally stopped for gas and went to look in the mirror I couldn't even see my face for all the butterflies. It took a while to clean up and the taste and smell wasn't so great either.

After I cleaned up, got gas and something to eat I headed home for the last stretch of my trip.

I made it home and then cleaned up the motorcycle and got myself a shower as well. In a few days I'd be going into the Army. My hair had gotten fairly long so the day before I had my dad give me a hair cut so it wouldn't be so long when I went in. Some friends stopped by my house to say goodbye, some of them I never saw again. Others I've kept in touch with still today.

Rose Parade

The New Years Rose Parade is truly an amazing experience, especially in person. I went there four times over the years. Three times in the late 60s and early 70s and one time in the early 80s with my wife, my brother, Brad, his wife and son, and his in-laws when I was visiting California. Two times I went there with our church group and once with a couple of friends from college, Dan and another friend, not sure of his name but I think it was Phil. We'd usually get there early and set up our sleeping bags on the sidewalk. There are lines painted on the road on Colorado Blvd that all have a special meaning. The first line on the sidewalk from the curb means that at 11:30 PM just before midnight on New Years Eve you can move up to it. I could be wrong about the exact times, but you get the idea. Of course at midnight every one's running around kissing and hugging and then moving their chairs, sleeping bags, rope barriers, etc. so they can claim their spot for the parade eight hours away. Sometimes you'd see girls sitting on the back of an open convertible and guys are running up and giving them kisses. I guess one guy got pissed off at his girl friend kissing all those guys that he put the top back up and made her get inside.

Of course the biggest and wildest part of the parade was watching all the cars and people going by all night long before the parade. Seeing all the cars going by was like watching a car show on TV. Some of these cars belonged on the cover of a magazine. Some would bounce up and down with their hydraulics, crazy horns, loud radios and sound systems, it was wild. There was always a truck with a sign and speaker proclaiming the end of the world is coming with a few religious fanatics hanging out on it. Then there were the guys, and girls, so loaded or stoned they could hardly walk, talk or see straight. Off the sidewalk in some of the parking lots people were getting sick, passing out and all kinds of stuff. Cops were arresting people and making people pour out their wine or booze if they were under age.

We would walk all the way to the start of the parade where all the floats were parked before they started the next morning. These were always amazing to see up close, much better than on TV, with all the flowers and organic materials and the exquisite details. It takes a whole year of planning and building these floats especially the animated ones. I went to Cal Poly, Pomona (California State Polytechnic College Pomona, for two years, later it was renamed from College to University) from 1969-1971. I helped put the finishing touches on the float one year as I was just one of the dozens of last minute volunteers they needed to help get it completed before it was to be transported to the start of the parade in Pasadena. Cal Poly always has a great float and usually wins best animated float or does very well. I was only able to help for a couple of hours but it was great seeing how it was put together and then seeing it in the parade knowing you had a small hand in it.

Seeing the Rose Parade on TV every year is something I always look forward to. The year I went with my two college friends was indeed a very interesting experience. After the parade was over it took about an hour to get out of the neighborhoods because of all the traffic. After being up all night I was really tired and found myself dozing a little. The guys were both totally zonked and soon I was too. I went over a center divider and blew out a tire and scraped the bottom of the car. I was very lucky that there was no pole or sign in the center divider like most of the others had.

Besides getting a flat tire, I fractured and broke off a piece of the exhaust manifold. Which made the car sound loud since the exhaust wasn't going through the pipes any more. Needless to say after changing the tire I was wide awake the rest of the way home. Later the next week I got a couple of new tires and found an exhaust manifold in a junk yard for $6. All in all I think I was very lucky that I didn't hit someone, or another car or run into anything. I've never fallen asleep driving since, no matter how tired I was because I always think of that time and how lucky I was.

A Road Called ZZYZX

On the road to Las Vegas about half way there is a road in the middle of nowhere near Baker, California that goes about one hundred feet on either side of it. It is called ZZYZX. I don't know if the road is still there and I don't know the significance of it but there it was. I did a Web Search once a few years ago just for the heck of it and found An International Trading Company in New York called ZZYZX. Now on the web are lots of web sites including one called zzyzx rd, there is even a zzyzx movie.

I just got on again and this is what I found on the web. Wow, this is the actual road that leads to a place called the Zzyzx Springs.

http://www.roadtripamerica.com/signs/zzyzx.htm

Here is the web site and the dialogue that is in it is included here.

"Ironic, we thought, that Pekka Helos sent RoadTrip America® a picture of this particular road sign. He sent the photograph via e-mail from Finland, and we received it in Nevada, not far from where it stands on the edge of Interstate 15, near Baker, California.

The arrow points south down a road that soon turns to sand and bends around a basalt outcropping to Zzyzx Springs, an old health resort started by a charismatic quack named Doc Springer in the early decades of the 1900s. A Los Angeles radio personality, Springer used the airwaves to drum up business, which, at the height of his career, was brisk. His resort might still be thriving today if he hadn't built his establishment on land he didn't own. Essentially a poacher, Doc Springer was eventually evicted, and his erstwhile spa is now used by biologists as a research station.

And so Doc Springer's real legacy is not a miracle cure or a vacation spot, but Zzyzx itself. The name he invented (which, by the way, rhymes with Isaacs) has never ceased arousing curiosity, and it's been appropriated by more than one science fiction writer. I, too, have fallen under its spell, and have used Zzyzx Road as a location in a novel."

29

painting by Bruno Turpin

67 Things You Must Do As a Surfer

I thought I'd just put this in because I thought it would be fun to hear what other people have done from this list. Let me know!

I bought an Oversized Collectors Edition of Surfer Magazine and one of the subjects they talked about are the 67 things you must do as a surfer before you kick out and ride your last wave. Meaning before you check out. Sort of like the movie "The Bucket List." I took a look at them and have counted about 43 of them that I've done. Not all are actually directly related to surfing but are closely associated with surfing or surfers. I thought it was a pretty cool list.

I'll list these 67 things and then the ones I did and when and where I did them, if I can remember the details, if not you'll have to take my word for it. (LOL). The funny thing is that most of these happen just during the course of surfing, the others you'd have to consciously set out to do. I doubt anyone has actually done them all by accident or even done them on purpose. But I'm sure most hard core surfers have done most. See how many of these you've actually done. It was fun trying to recall them. Mine are listed [between the square brackets].

The following is an excerpt from Surfer Magazine, Oversized Collector's Edition, August 2006, pages 182-201

The article is entitled "The Surfer's Life List: 67 Things Every Real Surfer Must Do Before Kicking Out"

1. **Make a pilgrimage**.

   Hawaii, The Gold Coast, Jeffreys Bay, G-Land . . . doesn't really matter where, so long as you get to one of surfings' holy grounds and post up until you've had your fill. And always leave your plane ticket open-ended.

photograph by Cec Forsyth
Andy Forsyth, Waikiki rental surfboard, 1973
[Mine was to Waikiki, Oahu, Hawaii, August 1973]

2. **Surf a contest.**

   If you think contests are just about competing, you're missing the point. They're about surfers gathering together from distant shores and celebrating being part of the tribe. So put on a pink jersey at least once and embarrass yourself. Or maybe even get through a couple of heats and build your self-esteem.

SURFING ADVENTURES
of the '60s, '70s and beyond . . .

photograph by Steve Wilkings
Tandem Surfing, Carlsbad Contest, 1965

[never got in a contest, but I've watched a few of them at Huntington Beach.]

3. **Name a spot.**

[never did this either, unless you count Leo Carillo State Beach in the surfer's area, I called it "Surfer's Paradise", my mom saw where I wrote on a photograph and that's what she titled the painting she did of Leo Carillo.]

4. **Get a good surf shot of yourself.**

We all need a little proof that we surf. Plus it'll give you something to show the grandkids.

photograph by Jane Forsyth

[My mom took one of me at Leo Carillo at the end of a wave, and she also took a couple of others, these were the only surfing pictures of me, about the summer of 1970 and 1971]

5. **Get chased out of the water by lightning.**

   [Huntington Beach 1969]

6. **Look like an addict.**

   Boss starting to question those bloodshot eyes, those unsightly scabs on your neck, that water dripping from your nose?

photograph by Jane Forsyth

   [Almost always during the summers of 1969, '70 and '71]

7. **Drop in on a surf star.**

   Tip of the cap to the pros of the world, but there's sweet righteousness in cutting them down to size. Hey, they're just surfers.

   [nope]

SURFING ADVENTURES
of the '60s, '70s and beyond...

8. Disappear.

painting by Garry Birdsall

Bus to Nowhere

A surf trip isn't serious unless at some point you fall off the map, no phone, no email, no itinerary, no nothing. Spend some time at a spot where it would take weeks for someone to find you if you died. At least you'll leave behind a smiling corpse.

photograph by Steve Wilkings

Mexico K-38, 1965

[Spring Break, 1970, Ensenada, Mexico]

9. **Impress the natives.**

You too can be as beloved as Indiana Jones. Get out there far enough and your talents on a surfboard, however weak, will turn you into a celebrity. Just hope the chief's daughter is hot.

[nope]

10. **Go 5-star.**

Admitting you like fluffy pillow, warm showers, multi-course meals and ice in your drinks does not make you less of a surfer, just a puss. It's not as hip as camping in the mud, but let's be honest, a ritzy hotel overlooking the surf has its perks. Don't make a habit out of it, but do it at lease once.

photograph by Brad and Colleen Forsyth, 2008

[Oahu, Hawaii, 1973, (Outrigger East Hotel, the Penthouse), Lihue, Kauai (Kauai Resort Hotel]

11. **Invent a new maneuver.**

[1969, Passing over the top of another surfer when they are at the bottom, basically creating a wake that takes them out of the wave, which they shouldn't have been on anyway since I had position, my surfing friends called it the Irish Ax]

SURFING ADVENTURES
of the '60s, '70s and beyond . . .

12. Shape your own board.

[never had the opportunity]

13. Get shacked.

It doesn't have to be bigger than your room, just bigger than your bathroom.

[Newport, 1969]

14. Use your surf status to get lucky.

There are potent phenomes in that smelly wet suit, and at some point the sandy feet, sun-bleached hair and tanned skin will be regarded as an aphrodisiac by a certain someone. How you cash in is your business.

[1969-1971, nuff said]

15. Freeze your ass off.

Sadly, some of the world's best waves lie in cold, inhospitable places. Grab a parka, dry suit and some 7 mm booties and jump in . . . it only hurts for the first five minutes. (by then you're too numb to feel anything)

[not really, but I did go surfing in the winter a lot at Balsa Chica, once on New Years day]

16. Go leashless.

[We didn't have leashes, I only used one once in 1985 at Ocean City, MD]

17. Spin a good yarn.

It is your duty to keep surfing's oral history alive, even if that means making shit up. The more you share a story, the better—and longer—it should get. That's why geezers always tell the best tales.

[sort of like this book, cause everything in here I've told many times over]

18. Surf with dolphins.

And realize what a kook you really are.

[Dolphins, porpoises, otters, seals, and even sharks <look out!>, I even talked to an otter once for about a minute at Leo Carillo, he didn't say much]

drawing by Jane Forsyth

internet open source

19. Get interviewed by Curious Gabe.

[Never met the man]

20. See a surf movie in a packed theater.

[Only on Video or DVD at home]

21. Go tandem.

photograph by Steve Wilkings

[I would've like to, with you-know-who.]

22. Go retro.

Paying homage to where we've been as a culture doesn't make you a poseur. In fact, there's a good chance you'll tap into something new. Find an old shape—whether a garage-sale special or a mint-conditioned replica—leave the leash and wet suit at home, and decide for yourself whether it really was better "back in the day."

[That's all I did back then, was retro, which for me back then was "now."]

23. Hike in.

Surf a spot that requires at least a one-hour hike in.

[At Leo Carillo it was about a ten-minute walk, doesn't really qualify.]

24. Eat shit.

And consider it dues paid.

[Everyone has, that has surfed serious waves]

25. Teach somebody to surf.

Use caution here. Remember that people who get bitten by the surf bug have been known to change religions, lose fortunes, and abandon their families.

[I tried to teach my brother, he never really got the hang of it. I also tried to teach Pete to surf.]

26. Surf in the rain.

[Many times in the rain, in the fog, with ashes falling.]

27. Paddle for the wrong wave on a huge day.

[Yep, many times, then you eat shit.]

28. Walk the nose.

photograph by Steve Wilkings

SURFING ADVENTURES
of the '60s, '70s and beyond . . .

painting by Bruno Turpin

[Huntington the most, San Clemente, pretty much most places.]

29. Surf a tropical reef pass.

[Can't say that I have.]

30. Make a wrong turn.

It's where most good surf stories begin. When it happens, you'll know it.

[Oh, yea, also many times.]

31. Get nailed by sneaker set.

Go on. Take your beating. Then paddle back out.

[More than once]

32. Drive the coast.

Age doesn't bring wisdom, miles do. And the hard miles, more than any other, are keys to self-discovery. Get on the road.

[1970, Ensenada, Mexico]

33. Meet a legend.

Lucky for you there's no pulpit separating the laymen from the clergy in surfing. Mixing it up with our heroes is easy. Just be cool.

internet open source

[Jeff Clark, August 2007]

34. Destroy the lip.

Stop aiming for the shoulder with those timid bottom turns. Nut up, square off, and aim high.

[San Clemente, summer 1971, with my short board]

35. Surf alone.

[Several times each year from 1968 to 1971]

36. Come to the rescue.

Bail your buddy out of that Tijuana jail. Feed a stranger's meter. Save a board from the rocks. Pull a tourist from a rip. It'll make you feel less guilty about the sport's selfish underbelly.

[Helped more that one person after a wipeout to get back to their board or get their board back to them.]

SURFING ADVENTURES
of the '60s, '70s and beyond . . .

37. Pay a bribe.

If you're doing things right, you'll eventually end up in a jam. Whether it's a federale or a greedy baggage handler, don't be afraid to buy your way out of it.

[What, me pay a bribe? actually I never did, I guess I'm doing something wrong.]

38. Earn a spot in the lineup.

We're not recommending that you paddle to the center of the pack and start thumping your chest—or somebody else's. Instead, just quietly devote yourself to a single surf break until you've earned a spot in the rotation.

[Leo Carillo, 1968-1971, 1973]

39. Get yourself fired.

At some point, that monthly contribution to your 401K won't stand up to a sweet 4' swell at 20 seconds pulse moving up from New Zealand. You can always get another job, but that swell will only last a few days.

[Fired from Taco Bell, 1968, but kind of indirectly, I was late one too many times after a day of surfing.]

40. Find a wall hanger.

No, not that poster of those dogs playing poker, but a small piece of surf history. If we don't protect this stuff it'll just disappear, says Dick Metz of the Surfing Heritage Foundation. Just remember, you can't buy your way into being a surfer.

[Nope, I've seen a few in surf shops, maybe one day I will.]

41. Kill your own dinner.

Tap into your inner caveman, slaughter a pig, behead a chicken, reel in a big one. It's better than jumping on the table, beating your chest and doing the Tarzan call.

[Fishing at Leo Carillo, 1967 (Rock Bass), Sacramento River, 1970 (Catfish)]

42. Do Waikiki.

photograph by Cec Forsyth

Waikiki, 1973, I'm out there somewhere. Diamond Head in the distance.

No, you're not too cool for this. Trust us, it's the birthplace of it all, and despite the hordes of pasty white buoys floating by, you'll be surprised by how available the original thrill still is. And you'll understand why Duke was king.

[August 1973]

SURFING ADVENTURES
of the '60s, '70s and beyond . . .

43. Surf an outer reef.

You've stared at that thing long enough on those big days. Yes it's rideable. Grab a buddy, grab your board, grab your balls, or your ovaries, and get out there.

[never got there]

44. Acquire a quiver.

You don't really need those schoolbooks, that retirement fund, or that anniversary present, do you? Warm your soul instead by hanging a new hybrid in the garage. The man who has a board for every condition has everything he needs.

[Only had 3 boards, Royal Hawaiin, 9'2", Hobbie 8'6", and a custom 7'0".]

45. Break a board.

Then milk it. Wow your buds, your girlfriend, your teacher. It'll ease the pain when you order a new one.

[Never broke a board.]

46. Stump your doctor.

They love a good challenge. Contract a tropical disease he's never seen before and you'll make his month.

[Just cut my foot open once, maybe it made his day?]

47. Become a dude.

For one week, at least embrace your inner Spicoli. Stop shampooing rub your stomach beneath your shirt, call your wife "bro" and talk about nothing but waves.

photograph by Jane Forsyth

[Leo Carillo, summer of 1970, didn't shampoo, bath, comb my hair, brush my teeth for the whole week, felt great.]

48. Take a road trip.

[just to Ensenado, Mexico, 1970]

49. Fix a ding.

[Fiberglass patch many times.]

50. Get a battle scar.

Best of course if you lacerate your back on a reef or take a fin to the face after pulling into a slab, However if you rip open your toe in the parking lot, just be prepared to lie.

[Balsa Chico, 1970, cut foot on glass bottle after jumping off my board. Cardiff-by-the-Sea got my wrist caught in a small crack in my fin and ripped open the skin that ended up leaving a scar. 1971]

SURFING ADVENTURES
of the '60s, '70s and beyond . . .

51. Make a movie.

[Wish I had a movie camera back then, when I was surfing in Dona, Kaui, Hawaii, someone was filming me. He never sent me a copy of the film.]

52. Get spit out.

There's making a tube, then there's being shot out of a tube. The latter rules.

[That would've been awesome.]

53. Surf at night.

There's only one way to make sure you're night life isn't getting in the way of your surfing. Just combine the two, it's fun as hell when you're in the tropics.

photograph by Steve Wilkings

[San Clemente, 1970 and Cardiff-by-the-Sea, 1969]

54. Surf with your family.

[My brother Chris, one time 1970 at Leo Carillo]

55. Launch one.

Face it. Flying is fun. Even more so if you know how to land. Age is not an excuse for copping out on this one. See what the rage is about.

[San Clemente, 1970, 1971, Huntington Beach and Leo Carillo]

56. Surf with a hero.

[Nope]

57. Carve.

[San Clemente, 1970, 1971, Huntington Beach and Leo Carillo]

58. Boat in.

[Nope]

59. Take a boat trip.

[1968 to Catalina with our High School Surf and Ski club]

60. Give a good wave to a stranger.

[Many times]

61. Watch the Pipe Master from the beach.

[I can only dream of this one, but I have seen it on ESPN]

62. Upgrade your surf spot.

[All the time.]

63. Go green.

Relax. You don't have to move into a redwood tree or rock hemp underwear. Just become aware of your footprint and do something about it. Pick up trash after a session. Send a check to Surfrider. Write a letter to the mayor about beach access. Do Something.

[I'd say I've done some of these, I always clean up my trash, even when camping.]

64. Score on Christmas Day.

[Too busy opening presents]

65. Get shown up by a grom.

There's profit in the humility that derives from watching a 10-year-old make a wave that would have kicked your aging ass. It happens eventually to all of us, so you might as well get it done now.

[Oh, I'd say more than once.]

66. Camp in the dirt.

It's softer than a waterbed and the sound of nearby surf will put any insomniac to sleep. Sex, however, can be gritty.

[Cardiff-by-the-Sea, 1968, 1969]

67. Hang 10.

Think you can't cheat nature? Think again. Hanging 10 toes both defies gravity and slows time.

painting by Bruno Turpin

[Huntington Beach and San Clemente 1970 and 1971 at least]

~~~~~~

So there it is. I've checked off 43 of these. How about you? If you can find this magazine it is great, one of the best I've ever purchased, great shots, lots of history and stories. Which I could've used some of the pictures and stories in this book. Feel free to email me with your list of the 67 Things you've done or if you just want to just comment on this book. Andy Forsyth:

alf000777@yahoo.com

30

painting by Bruno Turpin

Surfing Locations

    There are literally dozens of new surfing locations discovered every year it seems. With people traveling the world, improved technology, places that weren't even considered as surf locations are now on the surfing map. Although some are only surfable when the conditions are just right or certain times of the year. Besides the normal and well known places in Hawaii, Australia, California, Mexico, Africa, and the East, there are new places being discovered in South America, Europe or just in the middle of the ocean near a lonely island or shallow reef. An example of that is Maverick's at Half Moon Bay in Northern California near San Francisco, or Teaupoo, Tahiti or Peahi, Maui, Cortes Bank, west of San Diego, Outside Log Cabins, Todos Santos, Baja, or the Dungeons near Australlia. These are just a few of the Big wave places that have surfaced in the last 10 to 15 years. Of course the conditions have to be right with the wave traveling in the right direction but when the conditions are right then the surf is amazing. But big wave spots aren't the only new locations. There are plenty of medium size surf spots that are being discovered all the time. I remember a line in the movie ***The Endless Summer*** where Bruce Brown says, "If you had enough time and money you could travel the world surfing a different spot everyday for 50 years." No one has that amount of time obviously but with all the people around the world surfing now and passing on their new finds online with pictures and stories then you have the ability to find all those locations that Bruce was talking about and pick the ones you'd like to go to. Probably the most popular surfing location still has to be Hawaii because it has so many great surfing locations all close to each other and you can surf all year round.

There have been lots of surfing movies out telling their stories of great surfing locations. Even though there were a few movies made in the late 50s and early 60s the movie that launched massive interest in surfing was ***The Endless Summer***. Sure the Hollywood movies generated a lot of interest too but most hard core surfers didn't take these movies too seriously because the actors weren't even out there surfing for the most part. The films that showed them surfing were mostly just clips of real surfers edited in.

Surfing in Hawaii is mainly focused in and around Oahu at Waikiki, Makaha and the north Shore, along with Sunset, Pipeline and Waimea bay. There are other places but these are the most popular ones.

Kauai has some nice surf spots as well as the big island of Hawaii. North of Maui is a place called Jaws at Peahi, Maui. These waves can break at 30-70' plus when the conditions are right. Storms in the Pacific generate these huge waves and with the hi-tech capabilities today combined with the use of sonar buoys they can tell when and where these large wave conditions are likely to occur and the approximate size of the waves. Using this information the giant wave chasers can call up their surfing team and get everyone together including the film crew to start surfing and filming the waves and the action usually within 24 hours or less.

A list of known surfing locations can be found at the following web site. This is not the definitive list but it does have a lot of the best surfing locations in the world and it is always being updated.

The web site below has lots of surfing locations and you can get more details about each place, including a little history about the place and local information, hotels and other links. Here are some of the ones on the web site at the time of publication. More are being added all the time.

http://en.wikipedia.org/wiki/list_of_surfing_areas

SURFING ADVENTURES
of the '60s, '70s and beyond...

Africa

South Africa

>Amanzimtoti, Cape St. Francis (Seal Point), Durban, Jeffreys Bay, Mossel Bay, Muizenberg, Port Alfred, Port Elizabeth, Scottburgh

Morocco

>Essaouira, Taghazout

Asia

Philippines

>Aurora, Catanduanes, La Union, Oriental Negros, Pagudpud, Samar, Siargao, Zambales

Japan

>Hyūga, Kujukuri Beach, Minamisōma, Ōarai, Sendai, Shōnan, Tahara, Tōyō

India

>Goa, Indian Coast
>Kovalam Beach, Kerala, South India

Indonesia

>Bali, Mentawai Islands, Sorake Bay, Nias Island, North Sumatra

Sri Lanka

South Coast

>Hikkaduwa, Matara

Southeast Coast

>Arugam Bay

East Coast

>Trincomalee

Thailand

>Phuket

Oceania

Australia

New South Wales

North Coast, New South Wales

>Angourie, Ballina, Byron Bay(The Wreck), Byron Bay(The Pass), Coffs Harbour, Crescent Head, Duranbah, Fingal Head, Kingscliff, Lennox Head, Old Bar, South West Rocks

Newcastle Stretch

Sydney

Northern Beaches

>Avalon, Curl Curl, Dee Why, Manly, North Narrabeen, Palm Beach, Whale Beach,

Eastern Suburbs

>Bondi Beach, Bronte Beach, Maroubra Beach, Tamarama

SURFING ADVENTURES
of the '60s, '70s and beyond...

Cronulla

> Cronulla Beach, Elouera Beach, North Cronulla Beach, Shark Island, Wanda Beach

Wollongong

> Sandon Point

South Coast

> South Coast Pipe,

Queensland

Gold Coast

> 19th Avenue Palm Beach Palmy Army, Broadbeach, Burleigh Heads, Currumbin Alley—Alley Boys, Duranbah, Greenmount, Kirra Point Kirra Boardriders, Miami, Narrowneck Longboard Club, Sandpumping Jetty, Snapper Rocks Snapper Boardriders, Surfers Paradise, TOS (The Other Side Straddie)

Sunshine Coast

> Noosa Heads
>> Double Island Point, Noosa National Park, Sunshine Beach,
>
> Maroochydore
>> Alexandra Headland, Coolum
>
> Caloundra
>> Kings Beach
>
> Bribie Island

Victoria

> Torquay
>> Bells Beach, Jan Juc, Winkipop
>
> Phillip Island

Western Australia

Gnaraloo, Margaret River

South Australia

Kangaroo Island

Tasmania

Clifton Beach, Shipsterns

Hawaii

North Shore (Oahu)

Haleiwa, Laniakea, Off the Wall, Pipeline, Rocky Point, Sunset Beach, Velzyland, Waimea Bay

Other surf spots in Hawaii

Ala Moana, Oahu, Honolua Bay, Maui, Hookipa, Maui, Maalaea, Maui, Makaha, Oahu, Peahi (Jaws), Maui, Richardson Beach, Hawaii (island), Sandy Beach, Oahu, Shit Falls, Maui, S-Turns, Maui, Waikiki, Oahu, Windmills, Maui

New Zealand

North Island

Gisborne, Mount Maunganui, Piha, Raglan, Taranaki,

South Island

St. Clair, The Catlins

SURFING ADVENTURES
of the '60s, '70s and beyond...

Federated States of Micronesia

Palikir Pass, Pohnpei

Fiji

Cloudbreak, Tavarua, Restaurants, Tavarua

Tahiti

Teahupoo

Europe

France

Aquitaine—Anglet, Biarritz, Cap Breton, Cap-Ferret, Hossegor, Lacanau, le Lizay, Charente-Maritime

Norway

Bore, Rogaland.

Italy

Capo Mannu (Sardinia), Spiaggetta (Ostia), Varazze (Liguria)

Portugal

Coxos, Ericeira, Ribeira D'Ilhas, Foz do Lizandro, Pedra Branca, Peniche, Pico do Futuro, S.Julião.

Spain

North Coast—Mundaka(Biscay), Rodiles(Asturias), Xago (Asturias) Cádiz—Conil de la Frontera, Canary Islands—El Quemao (Lanzarote), Punta Blanca(Tenerife)

Great Britain

Cornwall—Bude, Crantock, Chapel Porth, Fistral Beach, Newquay, Perranporth, Porthtowan, Porthleven, St Agnes, Watergate Bay
Devon—Croyde, Lynmouth, Putsborough, Sandymouth, Saunton, Sennen, Westward Ho!, Woolacombe
Wales—Freshwater West, Llangennith, Llantwit Major, Newgale, Rhossili, Southerndown, St Davids, The Mumbles
North Yorkshire—Cayton Bay
Teesside—Saltburn
Lincolnshire—Sandilands,
Scotland—Aberdeen, Coldingham Bay, Fraserburgh, Pease Bay, The Bar, Thurso, Tiree
Challaborough

Ireland

Donegal Bay—Bundoran, Rossnowlagh,
County Mayo—Carrownisky, Louisberg, Keel Beach, Achill
Antrim—Portrush,
Kerry—Dingle Peninsula,
Co. Clare—Lahinch, Spanish Point

Greece

Aegean Sea

Poseidi, Chalkidiki
Golden Beach, Thassos
Agios Ioannis, Pelion
Kolimbithres, Tinos
Chorefto, Volos

Ionian Sea

Athens and Peloponnisos

Crete

Greek Islands

North America

Canada

West Coast

    Lawrencetown Beach and environs (Eastern Shore), Nova Scotia, Canada
    Tofino, British Columbia

East Coast

    Halifax County, Nova Scotia

Lachine Rapids

    Habitat '67 standing wave

Mexico

    Puerto Escondido, Oaxaca
    Baja California
        Isla Todos Santos
        Baja Malibu

USA

California

San Diego County, California
Black's Beach, Cardiff, Carlsbad, Del Mar, Imperial Beach, Oceanside, San Onofre State Park, Swamis, Windansea

Orange County, California
56th Street Newport Beach, Brooks Street Laguna Beach, Doheney Beach Dana Point, Trestles(near San Clemente), Huntington Beach, Salt Creek Dana Point, T-Street San Clemente, The Wedge Newport Beach

Los Angeles, California
El Porto Manhattan Beach, Haggardys, Hermosa Beach, Lunada Bay, Malibu, Manhattan Beach, Palos Verdes, Surfrider Beach, Topanga, Zuma

Santa Barbara, California
Campus Point, Leo Carillo State Park, Sandspit, Santa Cruz, The Ranch, Rincon

Santa Cruz, California
Mavericks Half Moon Bay, Pleasure Point, Steamer Lane

Pacific Northwest

Washington—La Push, Neah Bay, Westport

East Coast

New York—Davis Park, Gilgo Long Island, Long Beach,
Rhode Island—Narragansett,
New Hampshire—Hampton Beach
New Jersey—Cape May, Ocean City, Wildwood
Maryland—Ocean City
Delaware—Indian River Inlet
Virginia—Virginia Beach
The Outer Banks of North Carolina—C-Street Wrightsville Beach, Masonboro Island, Sand Dollar Shores, Shackleford Banks,
Florida—Cocoa Beach, New Smyrna Beach, Sebastian Inlet Brevard County

SURFING ADVENTURES
of the '60s, '70s and beyond...

Gulf Coast

Texas—Corpus Christi, Freeport, Galveston, South Padre Island
Florida—Anna Maria, Caladesi Islands, Clear Water, Laguna Beach, Panama City, S.T. Pete Beach

Great Lakes

Sheboygan, Wisconsin

Caribbean

Barbados—Maycocks, The Soup Bowl
Dominican Republic—Playa Bonita, Playa Encuentro
Puerto Rico—Aguadilla, Dome's, Isabela, Jobos, Maria's, Midless, Ramey, Rincón, Shacks, Steps, Surfer's, The Landing, Tres Palmas, Wilderness, Wishing Well

Central America

Costa Rica—Dominical, Jaco, Nosara, Playa Grande, Puerto Viejo de Limón, Tamarindo, Witch's Rock,
Playa Zunzal, El Salvador—Conchalio, La Punta Roca, Playa El Tunco, Playa El Zonte
San Juan del Sur, Nicaragua—El Remanso, Maderas, Popoyo, San Francisco Bay, Tola
Guatemala—Ocos, San Marcos,

South America

Chile

Chile—Pichilemu,

Peru

Peru—Cabo Blanco, Cerro Azul, Chicama, Pico Alto,

Brazil

RJ—Rio de Janeiro, Saquarema
SP—Ubatuba,
PE—Fernando de Noronha
SC—Garopaba, Joaquina, Praia Mole, Praia do Rosa
RS—Torres, Ilha dos Lobos
Pororoca, tidal bore on the Amazon river

Other South America

Galapagos Islands

31

drawing by Ashley Forsyth

Places I've Surfed

Newport Beach, 1967-1971
Corona Del Mar, 1967-1971
Huntington State Beach, Pier, 1966-1971
Huntington City Beach, 1967-1971
Leo Carillo State Beach, 1968-1971, 1973
Cardiff-by-the-Sea, 1968-1971
Malibu, 1968-1971
Sunset, 1968-1971
Long Beach, 1968-1971
Laguna, 1968-1971
Zuma, 1970-1971
Hermosa, 1969-1971
Redondo Beach, 1968-1971
San Diego, 1970
San Clemente, 1968-1971
Encenada, Mexico, 1970
Waikiki, Hawaii, 1973

Dana, Kauai, 1973
Ocean City, MD, 1985
Indian River Inlet, MD, 1985
Note: The dates of 1966-1971 are my best recollections of when I surfed there. Sometimes I may have only surfed there one time, like at Laguna but I don't remember the exact year, probably 1970.

Places I've watched surfers but wasn't able to surf:

Galveston, Texas, 2006
Santa Cruz, Half Moon Bay, 2007
Daytona Beach, Florida, 1992
Hawaii, Big Island, 1973

Author's Final Note of Thanks

I'd like to thank you for taking the time to read this book. I hope it has inspired you to take a renewed interest in surfing. I also hope you have enjoyed some of the humor, craziness in the stories here and that it took you back to a wonderful and amazing time when we were out there surfing, having fun and just enjoying life at the beach or where ever we happened to be. I hope to hear from you with your stories about your surfing adventures. I'd really like to hear some more crazy surfing stories, I know they're out there.

Thanks again, Andy.

We Felt the Summer's Sun

The end is near
But I will not fear
A cold winter is coming
While the warm summer is leaving

Fall is our warning
Of dangers the ice brings
But the snow is a beauty
Begging us to enjoy

These summers left us memories
That never will pass our minds
Palm trees, water and surf
And freedom in our bones

And the cold wind
Blew us back again
Away from our dream
Awakened from a sleep with no pain

Four months will pass
The snow and ice will melt
A long time at last
Then we're back, to the sun and the surf we've felt

Andy 9/9/1973